Dublin's Victorian Houses

Edenvale Road, Ranelagh (Barry Mason)

Dublin's Victorian Houses

Mary Daly
Mona Hearn
Peter Pearson

A. & A. Farmar

Published by
A. & A. Farmar
Beech House
78 Ranelagh Village
Dublin 6
Ireland

Tel: + 353 1 496 3625 Fax: + 353 1 497 0107
Email: afarmar@iol.ie Web: www.farmarbooks.com

Published in association with Sherry FitzGerald

First published 1998

ISBN 1 899047 42 5

Text design and typesetting by A. & A. Farmar
Picture research by Peter Costello
Cover design by Cobalt
Cover photographs by Barry Mason
Origination by Accu-plate
Printed in Ireland by Betaprint

Contents

Publishers' Introduction

The second half of the nineteenth century saw an extraordinary development in Dublin. A series of self-governing townships were created—starting with Rathmines in 1847 and ending with Drumcondra in 1879—which positively boasted of their freedom from the normal constraints of local government, whether from the city of Dublin itself, or from the Local Government Board.

The new middle class flocked to these enclaves, where architects and builders developed new roads and streets filled with the characteristic sturdy red-brick houses. This book celebrates these houses. But to understand any house, we need to understand the social and economic background. What were the social and economic considerations that pushed development to one side of Dublin rather than another? Why was Pembroke grander and more spaciously laid out than Rathmines?

As well as being a social arena, even a status symbol, every house is also a more or less efficient machine for living in. These houses had to address certain practical goals; since all heat, whether for cooking, washing or warmth, had to come from fires, removing smoke was critical. Hence the architectural prominence of chimneys. Until the end of the century water for washing (not to mention human waste) had to be carried to and from bedrooms. Washing clothes was a dreaded weekly chore—so physically demanding that some physicians believed it shortened women's lives. Storing food in summer was a constant headache—housewives were advised to scrape the mould off mutton or beef regularly.

As far as housing was concerned, the Victorian age was a little late starting in Ireland. Rathmines did not become a township until 1847, and as late as 1853 Ranelagh was described as 'well sprinkled with villas' which hardly suggests intensive development. On the other hand it did not end with the death of the old Queen in 1901—indeed some argue that Ireland was essentially a Victorian society until the 1960s. So that while there is much that is very strange to modern eyes in these pages, there are also many aspects that will be familiar and instantly recognisable. As far as house design was concerned, it was not until 1907, with the exhibits (later built) at the International Exhibition, that a noticeably Edwardian style came to Dublin.

Illustration sources

Costello Collection: half-title, pages 2, 18 (top), 25 (top), 26, 37 (plan), 42, 60, 71, 86, 99, 110, 111; Alex Findlater: pages 63 (bottom), 117; Charles Horton: pages 81, 107, 113, 127, 129; Mona Hearn: page 68; Irish Architectural Archive: pages 31, 68; Irish Picture Library: page 80; Barry Mason: page 153; Peter Pearson: pages 3, 61, 90, 94, 114, 132, 134, 136, 137, 141, 142, 147, 148; other pictures from Sherry FitzGerald and A. & A. Farmar. Colour pictures as indicated.

A. & A. Farmar would like to acknowledge the assistance of Sherry FitzGerald with this publication

Tony and Anna Farmar
17 October 1998

The growth of Victorian Dublin

Mary Daly

One of Dublin's earliest photographs shows a street scene in the 1840s—
Victorian Dublin was just poised to take off.

Most Dubliners are extremely conscious of the city's Georgian housing but the much larger area of Victorian housing has attracted little interest until recent times. Although few Dubliners are likely to live or to have lived in a Georgian house, an estimated 35,000 families live today in a house that was built during Victoria's long reign.

During the nineteenth century most European cities expanded far beyond their existing boundaries. Dublin, which was one of the ten largest cities in Europe in 1800, grew at a much more modest rate than other capitals. When Queen Victoria came to the throne in 1837 there were still large tracts of undeveloped land in the territory bounded by the North and the South Circular Roads, though streets and terraces of houses were already being erected to the south of the Grand Canal which marked the southern boundary of the city, just as the Royal Canal marked its northern boundary. In 1901, the year of Victoria's death, the built-up area extended as far as Terenure and Kimmage and in the south-east to Ailesbury Road and the end of Sandymount Strand.

On the north-side, Glasnevin's Botanic Gardens were at the very edge of the city. Although Fairview was heavily built up, there were still large tracts of vacant land in Drumcondra. Griffith Avenue, for example, which is named after Arthur Griffith, was only developed in the 1920s, and the south-west part of the city in Dolphin's Barn and beyond still consisted of farmland and market gardens. Although Dublin and its suburbs had grown considerably during the previous fifty years, it was still possible to walk from the city centre to the outskirts.

The Respectable and Salubrious Suburbs

The story of Dublin's Victorian houses is very much a suburban story. In Dublin, as in English cities, though not in continental cities such as Paris, respectable families preferred to live in single-family houses, not in large city-centre apartments. Although there was quite an amount of undeveloped land within the city at the beginning of Victoria's reign, most of the new houses catering for middle-class families—particularly the more imposing houses—were built in the adjoining suburbs, such as Rathmines and Pembroke to the south, or Drumcondra and Clontarf to the north.

In the past, most city businessmen and professional men would have lived at their place of work, probably above the shop or workshop, though wives and children might have moved from the city to a country or a seaside cottage during the summer months. During the nineteenth century, however, those families that could afford to do so began to separate their residence from their place of work, and we see the beginnings of modern housing developments, which are exclusively residential. The aristocracy traditionally had a country and a town house; by moving to the suburbs the middle classes were aping this aristocratic practice, while still remaining close to their place of work. A suburban address also enabled a family to assert its respectability, because it implied a separation between work and family, between the private sphere of children and household, which was dominated by the woman, and the male world of business and employment.

Central Dublin contained many streets of Georgian housing that were originally built to provide town residences for the Anglo-Irish gentry. Quite a number of these would have been available for rent during the mid-nineteenth century. Some, like Henrietta Street, consisted of imposing mansions that were the former residences of the aristocracy or the highest ranking members of the legal profession. Although these would have been beyond the means of an average solicitor or businessman, there were less expensive Georgian houses to be found in Dominick Street, Pembroke Street and numerous other city addresses. Yet many of these houses, particularly on the north side of the city, fell into decay and were turned into tenements; others became dingy boarding-houses or were used for small businesses.

This is not to say that no respectable Victorian households occupied these older properties. The nationalist MPs John Dillon and David Sheehy lived in the north city, in North Great George's Street and Belvedere Place respectively, and the south-side Merrion and Fitzwilliam Squares were the homes of many of Dublin's leading doctors and lawyers. However, the only imposing houses that were built within the city boundaries during Victoria's reign are those in Earlsfort Terrace and Adelaide Road. Although Earlsfort Terrace was first opened up in 1839, most of the street was not developed until the 1870s. Efforts were made during the late 1830s to build a new square containing prestigious houses off Hatch Street, which was to have been called Wellington Square, but the development never took place. The long delay in building on this site, at a time when many expensive houses were being erected in suburban areas such as Rathmines and Pembroke, indicates that living in the city was no longer seen as fashionable.

Most of the houses that were erected adjoining the North and South Circular Roads were much more modest in scale and they were occupied by clerks and families who could not afford to be as selective about where they lived. There would never have been sufficient space within the city area to provide houses for all of Dublin's lawyers, civil servants, businessmen, doctors and clerks; the limited space available was used to build houses catering for families with lower incomes.

Why did so many Victorians prefer to live in the suburbs?

Dublin in 1837, the year Queen Victoria came to the throne. Expansion beyond the canals began in earnest some twenty years later. As late as 1853 Ranelagh was described as: 'a pretty outlet [to the country], well-sprinkled with villas' (W. F. Wakeman: 'Dublin—What's to be Seen and how to see it').

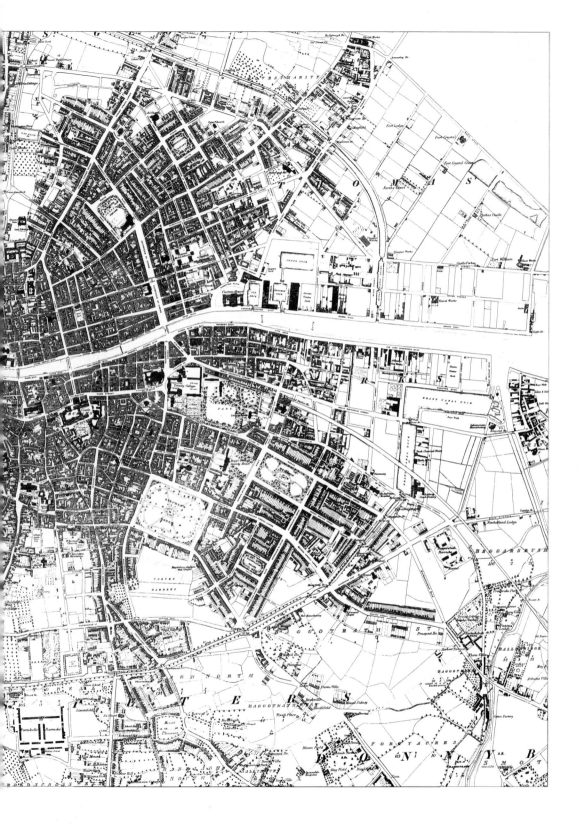

The typical middle-class Dublin family in Victorian times wished to live in a safe and healthy environment, in a home that was reasonably close to the man's place of work (almost no middle-class-women worked outside the home at this time), and as far as possible they sought a neighbourhood that contained people with similar interests and lifestyle and often a particular church or chapel. This was a major consideration in Victorian times and most new housing developments made provision for a church or a chapel and advertised this fact to prospective householders.

Today the majority of Irish families own their homes or at least aspire to do so. In Victorian times, however, the overwhelming majority of respectable families lived in rented houses. They moved house more easily than we do today. Tenement families flitted from one address to another, one step ahead of the bailiff and the debt-collector, and James Joyce's impecunious father moved his family through large tracts of the southern suburbs: Ontario Terrace, Rathmines; Brighton Square, Rathgar; Castlewood Avenue, Rathmines; Martello Terrace, Bray and Carysfort Avenue, Blackrock, until he was eventually forced to move to the north city with addresses at Hardwicke Street and Fitzgibbon Street. However, many families that were certainly not in financial straits also moved house at regular intervals, renting larger homes as the size of family increased or the household became more prosperous, or taking a seaside villa at Sandycove or Dalkey perhaps for the summer, or for a longer stay on medical advice.

There was no long-term rise in the price of houses during Victoria's reign, and consequently most householders did not expect to face a severe increase in rents, or to reap the benefits of capital gains from home ownership. Although house prices did rise during the middle of the century, in line with the overall price index, they fell slowly but steadily from the 1870s to the late 1890s. While the Dublin housing market went through

something of a boom during the 1860s when numerous three- and four-storey houses were erected in areas such as Rathmines, Pembroke, Clontarf and Blackrock, house-hunting does not seem to have caused major distress for the typical middle-class family. Dublin and its suburbs grew much more slowly during the nineteenth century than most British or continental cities, and most street directories indicate that there were substantial numbers of vacant houses at any time.

A Dublin tenement pictured at the end of the century. It is difficult to believe that such conditions actually represented an improvement in the living conditions of Dublin's poor over what was available in the early part of the century.

For this reason house owners had to be extremely conscious of the needs and the wishes of potential tenants. Public health was a major consideration. This is hardly surprising given that Dublin, in common with many cities in Britain and Europe, suffered from epidemics of cholera in 1831–32, 1848–49, 1853–54 and 1866. The year 1865 saw a serious outbreak of smallpox, and there were further smallpox epidemics in 1871 and in 1878. Other infectious diseases such as typhoid, scarlet fever and measles claimed many lives, particularly among children. A total of 568 children died as a result of a measles epidemic in 1899. A hot summer invariably brought masses of flies and hundreds of deaths from dysentery. In 1865, the year of the smallpox epidemic, the number of deaths in Dublin city rose by over 700, or 9 per cent; in 1866 cholera claimed a total of 1,186 lives. Most victims belonged to the city's labouring poor. During the years 1841–51 the death-rate in the first-class streets south of the Liffey was 0.81 per cent, less than one-third of the level of 2.64 per cent recorded in St Paul's Ward, a working-class area along the north bank of the Liffey.

However, middle-class households were not immune to premature death; five of the eight children of Sir Charles Cameron, the Dublin Medical Officer of Health and the leading authority on the city's public health problems, died either in childhood or early in adult life. Until the end of the nineteenth century the mechanism by which infectious diseases were transmitted was not properly understood, and it was widely believed, both by medical men and the general public, that they were spread by miasma—gases and vapours that rose from piles of rubbish and from human waste. Disease was associated with bad smells. Residents of the most exclusive city addresses, such as Merrion Square or Fitzwillliam Square were living within yards of squalid cottages, lanes and courtyards that were full of filth and disease. It is probably not a coincidence that Rathmines Township was established in 1847, when the Great Famine was at its peak, or that a record number of families migrated to the suburbs during the 1860s, a decade marked by epidemics of smallpox and cholera.

Moving to the suburbs did not entirely guarantee immunity from infectious diseases. It reduced the risk of contact with noxious smells and infected persons, but did not exclude the health risks posed by infected milk, dirty water and inadequate drains. In 1878 an outbreak of typhoid (which was generally associated with bad drains) in Clyde Road, Elgin Road and Raglan Road, claimed the life of Sarah Dale, wife of the leading Dublin accountant, Robert Gardner. In 1879 the same area suffered an outbreak of scarlet fever, which was eventually traced to infected milk. Despite these incidents, a suburban address probably reduced the risk of infection.

Health considerations ruled out housing developments in some parts of the city and suburbs. Families were not prepared to live beside a workhouse or a fever hospital, so this blighted large tracts of land in the south-west and the north-west of the city. Living close to a cemetery, whether Mount Jerome or Glasnevin, was also seen as posing a risk to health, and the continuous trek of cattle from Dublin's Broadstone Station and the cattle market at Smithfield towards the docks scarcely made living along this route seem an attractive option.

The dirt and smoke associated with railways meant that sites that were close to railway stations or railway lines tended either not to be developed, or they became the homes of the city's labouring class. Opposition from property owners in

Live cattle being driven to the North Circular Road market (and occasionally making a dashing bid for freedom) were a regular Dublin sight until the 1960s.

Kingstown, notably Thomas Gresham, the owner of Gresham's Terrace on the seafront, succeeded for some years in preventing the Dublin–Kingstown railway from running beyond Salthill. When the line was extended through Kingstown the railway company was required to keep both the track and the trains below ground level in order not to damage property values.

While Dublin was by no means an industrial city, the cluster of factories in the south-west of the city adjoining Guinness's Brewery meant that this area was not attractive for housing. The most fashionable roads in Pembroke were located at a safe distance from the small industries and the fishermen's cottages that clustered around Ringsend and, with the exception of Idrone Terrace that was built to capture a view of the sea, the larger houses in Blackrock were well removed from the village with its warren of crowded lanes, public houses and disease-ridden cottages.

Morality was another important consideration. All the military barracks in the Dublin area attracted the inevitable clusters of prostitutes, so it is no coincidence that the highest-quality housing in both Pembroke and Rathmines stop some distance from Beggar's Bush and Portobello Barracks. When prostitution associated with Portobello Barracks spread during the early 1870s into Kingsland Park, a city street that was close to Portobello Bridge, respectable families moved out, rents fell and houses remained vacant. Although the developer, Frederick Stokes, eventually succeeded in eradicating prostitution, the houses remained vacant, and in an effort to re-establish the area as a respectable address he changed the name to Victoria Street.

Property advertisements regularly boasted that the area in question was healthy. High ground was regarded as much better than low-lying sites. Advertisements often mentioned the type of soil on which the house was built. Well-drained gravelly soil was preferred to heavy clay; swampy land was seen as synonymous with fevers and infection. This explains why developers were slow to build quality housing in low-lying areas such as Fairview, parts of Clontarf, or the southern coast from Sandymount to Blackrock. Sea air was regarded as healthy, in part because it was believed to disperse all dangerous miasma. Many Victorian doctors, when confronted with a sick child or an ailing wife, often prescribed sea-bathing or a change of air, rather than acknowledge that they had no remedy to offer.

By the end of the eighteenth century some wealthy families rented houses along the coast for sea-bathing. Emily, Duchess of Leinster, packed off her innumerable children to live with a tutor at Frascati House in Blackrock. By Victoria's reign we find terraces such as Idrone sur Mer in Blackrock, St James's Terrace in Malahide and the many houses along the seafront at Kingstown (Dun Laoghaire) being erected to cash in on this fashion.

Moving from the city to the suburbs often made good financial sense. During the nineteenth century local taxes took a much larger share of a household's income than the direct taxes that were levied by central government. In Dublin city rates, which were usually paid by the occupier of a house (except in the case of small cottages and tenements), could amount to as much as one-quarter of the annual rent of a house. The charge was much lower in suburban areas because the poor rate covered the cost of maintaining paupers from an immediate area in the workhouse, together with other public health charges.

Most suburban areas did not contain a large population of impoverished families. By the 1870s a typical suburban householder faced a rates bill that was more than half that of somebody living in a similar house in the city. On the North Circular Road households living on the outer, i.e. the county side of the road, faced a rates bill that was one-third of that paid by the residents living on the city side. Dublin Corporation grumbled

Lower Albert Road, Sandycove

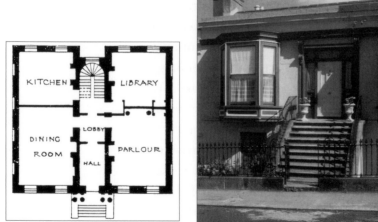

Clarinda Park, Dun Laoghaire

Although the earliest suburban terraces and villas predate Queen Victoria, they set a style that builders used until the 1880s. The basic plan was extremely simple and elegant.

that wealthy suburban residents often took advantage of the city's hospitals, fire brigade and other services that were paid by the city's ratepayers, without paying their fair share of the costs. However, suburban residents were not required to carry part of the city's tax bill until 1900 and there is little doubt that low taxes were a major encouragement for developers to build houses in the suburbs, and for families to take up residence there.

North side, south side

The earliest suburban terraces and streets were erected before Victoria came to the throne. Mountpleasant Square in Ranelagh dates from the 1830s and most of the main roads out of Dublin show a scatter of houses, much like the ribbon development on the outskirts of a modern country town. In Kingstown (Dun Laoghaire) the terraces on Crofton Road predate both the coming of the railway and Victoria's reign. As Dublin spread out beyond the canals, it took over the market gardens of Sallymount in Ranelagh and land along the Dodder where cattle had formerly grazed. Before areas like Ranelagh and Ballsbridge were covered in orderly roads and terraces, they contained isolated houses, some of them farm houses, or the country homes of wealthy city businessmen, while others provided cheap homes for the first generation of commuters. (During the seventeenth century Aungier Street was regarded as a suburb of the old city that huddled around the two cathedrals.) At the beginning of the nineteenth century Ballsbridge was an industrial village, with a large textile finishing plant. Remarkably, the Hammersmith Ironworks on Pembroke Road (at the site of the present Hume House and the Veterinary College) survived until the 1870s within yards of some of Dublin's most expensive houses.

In Clontarf, Monkstown and parts of Pembroke, however, cottages that had been the homes of fishermen and agricultural labourers were levelled to make way for bigger modern houses.

Evicting fishermen and cottiers seems to have been particularly common as a prelude to housing development in Clontarf. Although the new suburban areas were developed with the middle classes firmly in mind, pockets of working-class housing survived in places like Gulistan in Rathmines, in the old village of Williamstown (opposite Blackrock College), and in the ancient fishing and port villages of Ringsend and Irishtown.

The Victorian housing market went through phases of boom and slump, like the housing market today. The most sustained housing boom seems to have taken place in the 1860s. During that decade the boundaries of Rathmines Township were extended twice, first to include Rathgar and then to take in Harold's Cross. By the end of the 1860s the built-up area extended to the township boundary at Brighton Road. Suburbia had not spread much beyond that point by the early 1900s. Meanwhile, the area around Seapoint, Montpelier and Temple Hill, Blackrock, was being laid out in building plots, as were large sections of the Pembroke Estate. Kingstown was also growing rapidly.

Most of the first phase of Victorian housing was concentrated on the south side of the river Liffey. During the early eighteenth century, the most fashionable Dublin addresses were on the north side. However, in the middle of the century the Duke of Leinster decided to build a house (Leinster House) on Kildare Street, and he boasted that fashion would follow him south of the river. By the end of the century the most desirable houses were in the south-east of the city, around Leeson Street and Merrion Square. By the middle of the nineteenth century fashionable housing had spilled across the canal into Pembroke and Rathmines.

Fashion was not the only explanation for the slow pace of housing development on the north side of the city. All the roads leading north from the centre of the city were toll roads until the early 1860s. Every consignment of bricks, or any other commodity, and every carriage entering or leaving the city on these routes was forced to pay a toll; the only toll roads on the south of the city were in the Crumlin area. The development of the north side of the city and the adjoining suburbs was also seriously handicapped by the lengthy lawsuit that was conducted by the heirs of the Blessington Estate, which controlled the largest tracts of land to the north of Sackville Street. As a consequence most of the land adjoining Dorset Street and the North Circular Road could not be leased for development until the 1870s. By then the fashionable suburbs were firmly located on the south side of the city. Efforts to turn Clontarf into a north-side version of Pembroke were not helped by the fact that the route to the city passed through low-lying swampy land, close to the Dublin docks, past several factories.

Until the early 1870s, when falling price levels following the end of an economic boom brought housing construction almost to a halt, most of the new houses that were built catered for professional and for upper-middle-class families. Houses built during these years in areas such as Leeson Park, Pembroke, Monkstown or Clontarf were large, with imposing granite steps and wide streets. By this stage, however, it would appear that there were probably sufficient new houses available to meet the needs of Dublin's professional and upper-middle-class households, and the slow pace of economic development in the city during the later decades of the century meant that this market did not expand significantly.

Although some large houses were erected after the 1870s, such as Rathgar's Orwell Park, most of the new demand for houses now came from clerks and others living on more modest incomes. They tended to find houses in some of the streets of small red-brick houses that were erected off the North and South Circular Roads such as Glengariff Parade, Arnott Street and Lombard Street West, or in Harold's Cross, Ranelagh and

Eden Quay (top) and Sandymount Green (right) in the 1890s

Whether in the bustle of the city or the tranquillity of the suburbs, transport, especially the tram service, was critical.

Drumcondra. These houses were smaller, less elaborate, with one or two storeys rather than the three or four storeys that were characteristic of the 1860s; the streets tended to be narrower and the developers were less likely to provide open space for a park. However, these houses probably marked a major rise in living standards for lower-middle-class families who had often lived in better tenements before this time. In order to afford the rent families living in these houses often kept one or more lodgers until a son or daughter was old enough to take a job and to contribute to the family budget.

Trams and trains

Improvements in public transport play an important part in the story of Victorian housing, though because Dublin grew much more slowly than a typical English or Scottish city, most people continued to live reasonably close to the city centre. Many of the inhabitants of Rathmines, Pembroke and Drumcondra regularly walked to work. As they crossed the canal bridges that marked the boundary between city and suburb, they often passed washerwomen, gardeners and others who lived in the city's tenements walking into the suburbs to do their day's work. By the 1860s only the largest and the most extravagant new houses provided a mews where the family's horse (or horses) and carriage could be accommodated, together with living accommodation for a groom.

Trams were the most important form of suburban transport, but before they appeared in the 1870s, people could travel to the city by horse-drawn omnibus. In 1868 an advertisements in *The Irish Times* for building sites at Brighton Square and Garville Avenue in Rathgar, which was at this time at the very edge of the built-up area, emphasised that 'Mr. Wilson's omnibuses pass hourly south of Brighton Square'. By the late 1860s the centre of Rathmines was served by one omnibus every ten minutes at peak times, which suggests that there was already a steady flow of people travelling to and from the city. In Ranelagh, however, the service only ran at 45-minute intervals, and there appears to have been no omnibus service at all running to the north of Sackville Street (O'Connell Street), evidence that this area was as yet largely undeveloped.

During the 1860s there was an unsuccessful attempt to provide Rathmines with a railway link. The proposed line would have run to Rathfarnham and Rathcoole, and a later, even madder, plan proposed an extension to Poulaphouca! Three stations were planned for Rathmines Township and in order to placate property owners, who were afraid that house values along the line would plummet, the line through Rathmines was to be underground. (The first London underground passenger service opened in 1863.)

In 1872, however, the first regular horse-drawn tram service in the city was launched from Nelson's Pillar, Sackville Street, to Rathmines. By 1879 a tram left Rathmines every three and half minutes at peak time; in Donnybrook and Sandymount there was a tram every ten minutes, and public transport had reached Drumcondra. From 1896 horse-drawn trams were gradually replaced by electric trams. Many of the existing bus routes, particularly those with low numbers, such as the Number 3 or the Number 11, still follow much the same course as the tramlines did at the end of the nineteenth century. The bicycle also became popular during the 1890s, though at the beginning people rode bicycles only for sport and leisure, not as a means of getting to work. It was only after Victoria's death that people began to commute to work by bicycle.

The close links between transport services and housing development are most apparent when we realise that James Fitzgerald Lombard and his son-in-law William Martin Murphy (now best remembered for his role in the 1913 lock-out), who were the two major shareholders in the Dublin United Tram Company, which gained control of the city's tram services in 1879, had invested heavily in housing, both in Drumcondra Township and around the North and the South Circular Roads. Indeed the rapid growth of Drumcondra from the late 1870s seems to have been heavily dependent on the provision of regular public transport.

Development along the coast

Although many of the terraces and single houses adjoining the coast from Blackrock to Kingstown predated the coming of the railway (whose development deprived them of gardens running down to the sea), some of the landowners whose property adjoined the Dublin–Kingstown railway line anticipated that the railway would bring a major boost to house-building. According to the parliamentary inquiry that was set up to approve the proposed line of the railway (rather like a modern planning inquiry) a lot of the land along the line was already laid out as building sites, awaiting development. Three railways stations were opened on the lands owned by the Longford and de Vesci Estate in Kingstown and Monkstown, with the encouragement of the landlords. By the 1850s it was being claimed that the cost of renting a typical house in Kingstown had doubled over the past ten years, and many additional houses were erected within walking distance of the train stations during the 1850s and the 1860s.

In the long-term, however, the railways carried much smaller numbers of commuters than the tram service. Railway tickets were much more expensive than tram tickets, and the service was less frequent, in part because the numbers travelling did not justify a better service. By the 1870s the weekly cost of a return second-class season ticket to Kingstown amounted to more than one-third of a labourer's weekly wage; in other words a commuter rail ticket was more expensive than the cost of board and wages for a housemaid. Many families obviously decided that a house in Rathmines offered better value. Property development along the railway line petered out after the 1870s.

Matters were not helped by the fact that many of the ninety-nine year leases on the Longford and de Vesci Estate, the major landowners in the area, were due to expire at the beginning of the new century. This meant that anybody who built a house would be forced to pay a stiff increase in ground rents or surrender the property. By the mid-1880s rents of houses in Kingstown had fallen sharply, yet despite this there seem to have been more vacant houses than in suburbs that were closer to the city. Despite the lower rents, people on modest incomes who worked in Dublin, such as clerks, simply could not afford to live there. Many of the smaller two-storey houses common throughout Kingstown, in Mulgrave Terrace or Clarinda Park West were occupied by retired people, by widows or single women, or by men who were employed locally either in shipping, coal-importing or other activities related to the port.

In the Blackrock area quite a lot of land passed into institutional hands; the large tracts of land occupied by Blackrock College, the Dominican Convent at Sion Hill, or Carysfort Teacher Training College, which opened in the 1880s, suggest that there was only a limited demand for housing, otherwise the land would have been used for this more profitable purpose. In both Monkstown and Kingstown several large houses were turned into private schools; further evidence that property was comparatively cheap along the south coast of Dublin Bay.

The housing market along the Dublin–Kingstown line could be described as moderately successful. Seaside housing was already fashionable before the coming of the railways and there was a constant, if limited, market for summer houses from Blackrock to Killiney, and along the north shores of Dublin

Bay. Many Dublin families regularly rented a house along the coast during the summer months. Novelist Annie M. P. Smithson, whose family lived in Baggot Street, recalled summers in houses at Seapoint or in Howth, though on other occasions the family moved to stay with her grandparents who lived near Sandymount Strand. Most Victorian houses in Killiney and Dalkey were originally intended only for summer occupancy and the area attracted holidaymakers from Dublin and farther afield. Irish MP John Dillon first met his wife, Elizabeth Mathew, the daughter of a prominent London lawyer, when both were holidaying in Killiney. Page L. Dickinson, a Dublin writer who spent many summers in Killiney noted that

> In the early days of its rise to fame, about the middle of the nineteenth century it became popular as a summer resort for well-to-do Dublin families. It was not really residential until the last quarter of the century. It had no cohesion, no collective social life and its hill side was dotted with the houses of rich families who spent their summers there.

Dalkey, a town dating back to medieval times and an ancient port, had a larger permanent population, but many of the villa-style houses that were erected were designed as holiday residences. The driving force behind Dalkey becoming a township in 1863, which gave it power to levy a local rate and to provide public lighting and other services, was James Milo Burke, a hotelier and the owner of Dublin's Shelbourne Hotel, and two other hoteliers.

If comparatively few Dubliners were prepared to commute to and from Dalkey, Blackrock or Kingstown, almost nobody was prepared to live along the more isolated parts of the Dublin–Bray railway line (the Harcourt Street line) before the end of the century. The houses that E. H. Carson, the architect father of Sir Edward Carson, erected near Taney Church and the Dundrum railway station proved to be an isolated development. Mark Bentley, who was a very successful property developer around Brighton Square in Rathmines, seems to have lost a lot of money in his efforts to lease sites that he had developed in Foxrock during the 1860s, despite the fact that they adjoined the railway stations at Carrickmines and Stillorgan and his promise to lay on a regular omnibus service to Kingstown. The land passed into the hands of the insurance company to whom he had mortgaged the property.

It was not until the early twentieth century, when golf had become a fashionable sport and motor cars were coming into use, that Foxrock housing took off. By then, with the greater interest in private gardens the larger sites available proved an added attraction. William Dargan, who is generally regarded as the father of the Irish railways, was somewhat more successful in his housing investments in Bray, again because of the attractions of the seaside.

Middle-class families who had fallen on hard times, such as the Joyces or the family of Francie Fitzpatrick, in Somerville and Ross's novel, *The Real Charlotte*, could still cling to respectability by moving to Bray where rents were lower than in other suburbs. Albatross Villa, the house rented by the Fitzpatrick's was 'just saved from the artisan level by a tiny bow window on either side of the hall door', and 'by standing just outside the gate it was possible to descry, under the railway bridge, a small square of esplanade and sea'.

The high cost of rail fares meant that many of the houses in Kingstown, Monkstown and Bray were rented by people who did not need to travel into Dublin every day—pensioners, annuitants and widows. There were only limited job opportunities in nineteenth-century Ireland for labourers, for the sons and daughters of farmers and for the sons of the Anglo-Irish middle

Late-Victorian Bray

class. Many of the latter found careers in India or the colonies. Sometimes their wives and children returned to Ireland, either to attend school, or to avoid the unhealthy tropical climate, and although such colonial households were found in every Dublin suburb, they seem to have been particularly common along the south coast, probably because rents were somewhat lower than in areas that were closer to the city.

Most men who sought their fortunes in the colonies hoped to be in a position to retire in later middle-age, and they often took up residence in the seaside suburbs. For those who were forced to commute to work in the city, the Victorian rush hour seems to have been a more leisurely affair than today's. If the working hours for labourers, factory workers, servants and shop assistants were long, the middle-class lifestyle was much more leisurely. Senior civil servants seem to have arrived in their office around 10–10.30 in the morning, when the post had already been opened and sorted by a junior clerk, and they frequently left for home around 4.30 pm or so. Many businessmen appear to have operated to a similar timetable. Only four trams left Rathmines before 8.30 am and the peak service from Brighton Road, the very edge of the built-up city, started at 9 am. After the introduction of electric trams, the journey to the city centre probably took less time than today.

Planning and the great estates

Not all Dublin housing was built on a generous scale.

How were these housing developments planned? At the beginning of Victoria's reign most local authorities did not have the legal authority to lay down regulations for buildings, or for the development of their district. The development of the centre of Dublin in the late eighteenth century was controlled by the Wide Streets Commissioners, but this was a special body that had been established by the Irish Parliament. These powers passed to Dublin Corporation in 1849.

In 1834 Kingstown Town Commissioners had a private Act of Parliament passed, giving them power to regulate the width and layout of streets and the general alignment of buildings. This ensured that new houses would be built at a uniform distance from the road, not jutting out in an irregular fashion. However, in most instances it was either the landowner (i.e. the landlord) or a lessee who determined the width and general direction of road; whether plots were laid out in a grid, a crescent or a square; the size of individual sites, the distance between houses and the road, and whether or not a park would be provided. The more winding streets followed the paths taken by traditional country roads or lanes.

The land surrounding Dublin city was owned by a variety of landowners. The largest single tract belonged to the Pembroke Estate; this extended from Merrion Square to Blackrock and then to Mount Merrion. Other landed families, such as the Earl of Meath, the Earl of Longford, Viscount de Vesci and Lord Palmerston all owned land. In some cases, such as the Pembroke Estate or the Palmerston Estate, responsibility for the actual development often rested with the agent: the land agent or estate agent, who managed a landlord's properties, whether in the country or in town and city, collecting rents and negotiating leases. Stewart and Kincaid, the firm of agents that managed the Palmerston Estate in Co. Sligo, also took charge

Palmerston Road, Rathmines (Barry Mason)

Beechwood Avenue Ranelagh (Barry Mason)

Lansdowne Road, Ballsbridge

Grosvenor Square, Rathmines

St Lawrence Road, Clontarf

Usually developers built the large houses in a township first

of the estate's property in Rathmines. This is the origin of the modern term estate agent, which is now taken to mean a person or a firm that is engaged in buying, selling and leasing property. By the end of the century as farmers came to own their land, the traditional role of the estate agent as rent collector fell into decline, and the term gradually came to assume its modern meaning.

The process of development was generally divided between two or three parties. Some landowners were extremely passive, simply opting to let the land to a developer on a long lease, without specifying precisely the manner in which it should be developed. More active landlords and their agents laid out the actual roads and the individual plots and then negotiated with prospective builders. In such cases the building leases often set specifications for the houses to be erected that were as stringent, and perhaps more stringent, than modern planning regulations. However, only landlords who owned property in the most attractive and most profitable locations, i.e. to the south-east of the city, who were also sufficiently wealthy to forego the immediate profits, could really dictate to developers in this manner.

The classic example of landlord control in the Dublin area is the Pembroke Estate in Ballsbridge, which was typical of the great English aristocratic housing estates, such as the Duke of Westminster's Belgravia, in insisting on high standards, even if this meant that the estate gained less revenue in the short-term. Ground rents on the Pembroke Estate were extremely high, much higher than in nearby Rathmines, and initially leases were only granted for ninety-nine years, though this was later extended to 150 years. In Rathmines it was generally possible to get a lease for 500 or 900 years. However, the estate agent claimed, probably with justification, that most of the initial income from ground rents was invested in the estate, in the form of high-quality roads, footpaths and other facilities. The estate was investing for long-term prosperity and it expected to profit when the leases fell in and the houses reverted to the estate. A typical lease on the Pembroke Estate required that the plans for the house should be approved by the estate and specified what building materials were permissible. Unfinished building sites were not permitted, a developer was penalised if the house or houses were not completed within a specified time. Leaseholders and house tenants were forced to observe lengthy covenants; clauses required that houses be kept in good repair, and properties could not be used for any commercial activity, whether this was keeping cows or butchering animals, or more innocuous activities such as running a school. Only a prosperous landlord, with land in a very desirable neighbourhood, could afford to be so selective.

The Longford de Vesci Estate in Kingstown fell on hard times in the early nineteenth century and, in order to raise some necessary capital, it granted numerous ninety-nine year leases on very liberal terms, without imposing controls on future development. Some of the consequences of this remain evident today in the higgledy-piggledy streetscape on York Road (some actually at right-angles to the road), and in the variety of street frontages and road widths that can still be seen along parts of Seapoint Avenue (Dun Laoghaire Corporation made some efforts to remedy this in the 1930s). When the finances of the Longford De Vesci Estate improved during the 1830s it succeeded in buying back some of these leases. The high standards of housing and the elegant lay-out of de Vesci Terrace and Vesey Terrace (both family names), reflect the benefit of the stringent regulations imposed by the estate.

The high standards required by the Pembroke Estate probably deterred some developers, so the population of the area expanded much more slowly than in adjoining Rathmines, and the standards set by the estate meant that it was not profitable to build smaller and less expensive houses, though the estate did provide some labourers' cottages. When the Vernon family, who owned most of the land in the Clontarf area, attempted to enforce similarly-high standards, they were less successful, because the area was less fashionable. For its part the Pembroke Estate showed no sense of urgency about leasing its land to developers: it was prepared to bide its time until the right offers came along. Building sites in Rathmines were advertised regularly in the Dublin newspapers; by contrast no advertisements ever appeared for sites in Pembroke. As the agent, John Vernon remarked, 'If builders tell me they will build, I lay out the road, but not until then.'

As a consequence, it took up to ten years (1845–55) before all the sites along Wellington Road were covered with houses. A similarly leisurely pace of development is also evident on the land belonging to the Palmerston Estate, another aristocratic estate at Rathmines. Most of the houses on Palmerston Road date from the 1860s; however, it was not until the early twentieth century that houses on adjoining roads like Cowper Gardens were completed.

The average landowner in the Dublin area could not afford to be so passive. Much of the land in Rathmines was owned by men who were less concerned at the estate that their grandchildren might inherit, and more determined to extract an immediate profit. Consequently, sites in Rathmines were advertised extensively; leases were generally issued for long periods—up to 900 years was common; ground rents tended to be lower, and leases were less stringent than in Pembroke. This is not to say that areas such as Kenilworth Square, which was developed by Michael Murphy, or Leeson Park, the work of Yorkshire-born Frederick Stokes, did not meet standards as high as those in Pembroke.

In all these cases building sites were prepared, roads laid out; perhaps a site was retained for a church or for pleasure grounds (the term that was commonly used at this time). Then came the actual building. In contrast to a modern suburban estate, where one builder might erect fifty or a hundred houses, the scale of construction in Victorian Dublin was modest—a developer might erect a terrace of six or eight houses; perhaps two pairs of semi-detached houses. Even a longer terrace, such as the seventeen identical houses on the north side of Belgrave Square in Monkstown, was built in blocks of two or three, over an eight to ten-year period. Surprisingly, in this instance the houses at either end of the terrace were the first erected; the last houses to be completed were in the middle of the terrace. In this case,

Blackrock Park. The park or 'pleasure ground' was an important amenity, providing a respectable excuse for women and children to get out of the house.

[31]

as in others, uniformity of design was guaranteed by the lease, which specified the width of each house, the distance from the road and the overall design of the houses. Each lease contained a tiny sketch of the prescribed doors and windows; this practice was also common on the Pembroke Estate.

In the case of longer roads, such as Palmerston Park, Rathmines, or Leeson Park, it is easy to spot the individual terraces or groups of houses that went to comprise the whole. Many roads that appear remarkably harmonious and uniform today were built bit by bit, often over many years; small details of finish distinguish one from another. The slow pace of development is not altogether surprising. As we already noted, Dublin city was not exactly booming during the latter half of the nineteenth century, so the market for houses was limited and it was often in a depressed state. More importantly, houses at this time were built to be rented, not built for immediate sale, so that capital was tied up for a much longer period than it would be today. For that reason, although some developers built large numbers of houses, they often did so in twos, threes or sixes, not in blocks of fifty or more. This enabled them to gauge the market; it may also reflect the fact that they could only afford to finance a small number of houses at any time. In contrast to the modern builder, who would expect to sell off a house within weeks or months of construction, whoever built these Victorian houses often held them for many years, so capital turned over much more slowly.

The developers

Who actually built the houses? Architects feature prominently in the list of names. E. H. Carson, father of the Unionist leader, Sir Edward Carson, was involved in building houses in areas such as Palmerston Road and Dunville Avenue in Rathmines, Marlborough Road, Donnybrook, on the Pembroke Estate, and, apparently less successfully in Dundrum. John McCurdy, the official architect to Trinity College Dublin, who designed both the Shelbourne Hotel and the Royal Marine Hotel at Kingstown, erected houses in Monkstown and Blackrock. John Hawkins Askin, a member of the architectural firm of Pugin and Askin, which designed numerous Gothic-revival churches throughout Ireland for the Roman Catholic Church, was a prominent developer in Pembroke Township.

However, many types of investors were attracted to the housing market. As we have seen, James Milo Burke, proprietor of the Shelbourne Hotel invested in houses in Dalkey. George Tickell, who owned one of Dublin's largest furniture warehouses, built houses in Clontarf—did he see the possibility of selling some of his furniture to the residents? Sir John Arnott, proprietor of the large department store and owner of *The Irish Times*, invested in property around the South Circular Road, including Arnott Street which bears his name.

Many of the houses erected during the 1870s in the vicinity of the North Circular Road and later in Drumcondra were financed by William Martin Murphy, the tramway proprietor who became owner of Clery's department store, his father-in-law James Lombard, and Irish nationalist MP and businessman Edward McMahon. By 1884 they had erected over 1,200 houses.

There were, of course, numerous smaller investors, such as clergymen, army officers and businessmen who wished to provide for their retirement. At a time when most people did not have occupational pensions, a typical husband and father was required to make some personal provision for his old age and for the support of his widow. He would also be expected to provide a dowry for his daughters, or an annuity in the event that they did not marry because middle-class women were not expected to be self-supporting. Housing was an investment that appeared to offer a secure and regular income; it often formed part of a personal investment portfolio together with other safe investments such as War Loan or railway shares. The parents of the executed 1916 leader Joseph Mary Plunkett lived exclusively on the rents of their Dublin house property. The dowry of his mother, Josephine Cranny, consisted of some of Marlborough Road; in later years the couple inherited more houses, all of them in the best parts of Dublin. According to their grand-daughter, the novelist Eilis Dillon, her mother confessed that 'when she was a child she could not imagine how it was to have a father who worked'.

The property pages of *The Irish Times* frequently listed sin-gle houses or small groups of houses for sale, but in contrast to modern-day property pages, these often tended to be invest-ment properties and the advertisements presented information on the possible income from the properties and not on the number of bedrooms or similar details. A businessman or a pro-fessional man might try to accumulate a small portfolio of houses to provide for his old age, much as somebody today builds up a pension fund. It was also quite common for a widow to be given a life-interest in several houses as part of her husband's will, or for a daughter's marriage settlement to make a similar provision. Houses were often willed to grandchildren, nephews or other relatives. Architects such as Carson probably sold some of the houses which they erected to clients as investments and continued to hold others as part of their own capital.

Water and sewage services

As we have seen, the prime role in determining the layout and design of these houses rested with the ground landlord. Once houses were complete, however, they needed certain services, such as water, sewers, and refuse collection. Many of the older houses would have drawn water from a well in their grounds (some of these still survive), and they might have made private arrangements for disposing of refuse and waste. However, as housing density increased such arrangements were no longer feasible.

An Act passed by Parliament in 1828 made it easy to establish a local authority with power to provide basic services such as public lighting, basic policing, paving and cleaning the streets, constructing sewers and drains, digging wells and providing water and keeping a fire engine. Any interested party could organise a public meeting with a view to establishing a township. All householders renting or owning property valued at more than £5 (i.e. bigger than a tiny cottage), were entitled to vote on the proposal. If they approved, the township would elect commissioners, who were required to be residents rated at £20 or more (i.e. a substantial house) and they would then take responsibility for setting a rate, hiring staff and organising street cleansing, water supplies and other services. This legislation, which was extended in 1854, permitted the commissioners to borrow money for improvements such as a water scheme.

The drains originally provided in suburban areas only carried away the surface water; night soil was collected in an ashpit in the back garden and it was carted away several times during the year. Modern sewers were gradually installed around 1880, though most domestic sewerage was simply emptied untreated into the river Liffey or Dublin Bay.

The 1828 and 1854 Acts provided Dublin suburbs with a form of local Home Rule. They were free to order their own affairs as they saw fit, with little interference from Dublin Castle, the Local Government Board in the Custom House, and most importantly in their eyes, Dublin Corporation. Rathmines was the first to take full advantage of this legislation, establishing its own township in 1847. In 1862 it was extended to include the areas of Sallymount and Rathgar; in 1866 it took in Harold's Cross and in 1880 it was extended to include Milltown.

Blackrock became a separate township in 1860; three years later the boundaries were extended to include Monkstown; Pembroke became a separate township in 1863, Dalkey in 1867 and Clontarf in 1869. Drumcondra, the last suburban township, which also included Glasnevin, was established in 1879.

The driving force behind these local authorities was generally the local landowners or local developers: in Pembroke and Clontarf it was the local landlord, the Earl of Pembroke and the Vernon family. John Edward Venables Vernon had a clause inserted in the legislation making him chairman for life; in Pembroke the chairman was invariably the agent of the Pembroke Estate. The pressure to include Monkstown in Blackrock Township came from the local builders, and from Stewart and Kincaid, the agents for the Longford de Vesci Estate. Rathmines was ruled in almost dictatorial fashion for its first thirty years by Frederick Stokes, an extensive property developer both in Rathmines and in the Portobello area of Dublin city. In both Kingstown and Dalkey, as we have seen, hoteliers played an important role, reflecting the fact that these towns were partly, if not primarily, tourist resorts, or watering places, to use the nineteenth-century term.

The lists of individual commissioners are dotted with the city's leading builders. E. H. Carson was a commissioner in both Pembroke and Rathmines. In Rathmines, where seats were rarely contested before the 1880s, anybody who erected a substantial number of houses was automatically invited to become a commissioner. The key figures in founding Drumcondra were J. F. Lombard, William Martin Murphy, James McMahon and local property owners including Dr Henry Gogarty, father of Oliver St John Gogarty, a successful Dublin physician who built houses on Botanic Road in Glasnevin. Lombard took steps to establish a township when alternative methods of organising a supply of running water for his houses had failed.

Clontarf Road, Clontarf

Fairfield Road, Rathgar

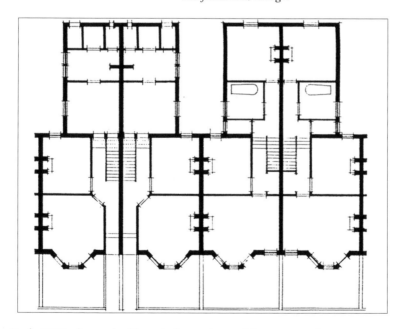

By the 1890s the standard bay window and ground floor entrance house was being built all over the suburbs. Above is a plan of a pair of houses (ground floor on the left, upper floor on the right).

In contrast to a modern developer, these men often retained ownership of the houses that they had built, and consequently they had a long-term interest in the area. They were often major ratepayers. Prospective tenants wanted value for money; they also wanted essential services such as water, refuse collection and public lighting. For the various commissioners it was often a matter of balancing the conflicting demands of economy and better services. In Pembroke the Earl and his agent seem to have continued to make most of the key decisions: the Pembroke Estate was more concerned with quality than with economy, and so low rates were not a major priority, though on one occasion an economy drive meant that all street lighting was cut off during the summer months. In Clontarf the Vernon Estate favoured economy, even though this probably stifled development: Clontarf lacked many basic services. Until it was incorporated into Dublin city in 1900 water supplies came from local wells.

In the case of Rathmines the commissioners regarded the commitment to keep the township rate at or below 2s (10p) in the £ as a major selling point and they were probably correct in this. However, the economy drive meant that Rathmines residents often suffered from poor services. Street crossings were not swept regularly and so Rathmines residents were forced to cross streets that were muddy and probably covered with horse droppings. This was a particular grievance for ladies with their long skirts. The sum set aside for the first Rathmines town hall was so paltry that the building soon collapsed; the thrifty commissioners recycled the building materials into the present town hall. Rathmines water came for many years from the Grand Canal—although the supply was inadequate and polluted it was apparently cheap; all the other suburban townships were supplied with Vartry water by Dublin Corporation. In a further effort to economise water was cut off at night during the summer months and water pressure was so low that houses on higher ground at the appropriately named Highfield Road and the adjacent section of Rathgar Road scarcely obtained any water at all.

In 1880 the town, with a population of almost 25,000, was without an effective fire brigade. Services improved gradually in response to protests from householders and during the 1880s Rathmines constructed its own water scheme at Glenasmole, which is still in use today.

The townships and Dublin Corporation

Self-government for Rathmines and Pembroke meant something more than saving money. The south-Dublin suburbs were something of a gilded ghetto to which Irish unionists could retreat; a place that they could control, and where they could live side-by-side with those who shared common political and religious values. Retaining a separate identity assumed increasing importance as tensions mounted over issues such as Home Rule; Dublin Corporation and Dublin city were to the forefront in the nationalist campaign. South Dublin and Trinity College were the only Irish parliamentary seats outside Ulster to return unionist MPs until 1918.

Most of the first-generation of suburban householders were Protestant. Although the majority came from an Anglo-Irish background, there was also a substantial sprinkling of recent migrants from Scotland and England who had come to Ireland to take senior positions either in the civil service, or in businesses such as insurance or railways. In 1911 one in eight of the adult population of Rathmines had been born in England or Scotland and one in eleven of the adult residents of Pembroke Township. There was also a substantial proportion of migrants from other parts of Ireland; Dubliners constituted a much smaller proportion of the population in the middle-class suburbs than in the city. Until 1901, the end of Victoria's reign, Catholics were a minority of the population of Rathmines and if we exclude the domestic servants, who were overwhelmingly Catholic (when the Church of the Three Patrons in Rathgar first opened in the 1860s it was commonly known as 'the maids' church'), it seems probable that a majority of Rathmines householders were Protestant at the outbreak of the First World War. Monkstown continued to have a majority Protestant population until the 1920s.

The predominance of Protestant householders in Pembroke, Rathmines and Monkstown is partly a reflection of the fact that these were middle-class communities, and Catholics were only beginning to gain access to well-paid jobs in the professions, the civil service and in business. However, suburbia also offered the Protestant Anglo-Irish a refuge from a city, and perhaps from a country, that was becoming more nationalist and more Catholic in its wider culture. According to Page Dickinson, 'The Roads', Clyde Road, Elgin Road, Morehampton Road and Pembroke Road were the homes of 'judges, colonels, leading lawyers and country gentry whose places were let; and many others of similar stratum. A pleasant enough society, whose common meeting-ground was the Castle, and the great Dublin houses, and the leading clubs of that time'.

Todd Andrews, who lived in Terenure as a child, claimed that 'Rathmines people represented for nearly all Dubliners the ultra-respectable section of the city with social aspirations disproportionate to their means'. The Rathmines accent was the butt of many Dublin jokes. Sydney Czira, who grew up in Rathmines, described it as a 'strange synthetic English accent'.

The differences between the suburbs and the wider Dublin population were expressed in various ways. Many Rathmines residents were strong supporters of the temperance movement and the local authority there, and in Clontarf, went to consider-

able efforts (with some success), to reduce the number of public houses in the area, by appealing against the granting of li-
cences. They also campaigned against Sunday opening. The li-
censing laws in Dublin city were much more liberal. Suburban
developments often came complete with a site for a church;
indeed the church or chapel appears to have been seen as an
attraction for potential residents and house-builders. Mark Bentley provided a site for the Methodist chapel at Rathgar's Brighton
Road; he also offered to provide a church on his unsuccessful
development at Foxrock. Sidney Herbert, heir to the Pembroke
Estate, brought over T. H. Wyatt, who had been the architect at
the family's church at Wilton in England, to design St
Bartholemew's Church in Clyde Road, which heralded the es-
tablishment of the new Pembroke Township. In Clontarf the
Vernon family erected a church in Seafield Road in 1864 as part
of their development strategy. The opening of Christchurch in
Leeson Park in 1862 was seen as enhancing one of the newest
and most prestigious suburbs at the time. Indeed the date when
a church was built or extended often provides an accurate guide
to the timing of housing development in an area.

Churches and chapels were more than places of worship.
Many people drew their friends from within the congregation.
Representatives of minority religions clustered in areas where
they were close to their place of worship and they could social-
ise with co-religionists. Many of the Society of Friends settled
in the Monkstown area within walking distance of the meet-
ing-house; the houses at Richmond Hill in Monkstown were
built by Quaker families. Presbyterians tended to live in Clontarf,
or in the adjacent Clonliffe area of Drumcondra. Methodists
also favoured Clontarf and Rathmines/Rathgar. Dublin's Jew-
ish families settled in the streets off the South Circular Road.
As they became more prosperous some families moved to
Harold's Cross and Rathmines, where they were still within

St Mary's Haddington Road was the richest Catholic parish in Dublin. The well-heeled parishioners lived in the 'Roads' of the Pembroke Estate. Their political allegiances can be gauged from the fact that this is the only Catholic church in Dublin with a memorial to its parishioners who fell in the First World War.

"ST MARY'S" HADDINGTON ROAD, DUBLIN.   215894.J.V.

walking distance of the synagogue at Adelaide Road and the original community.

The cosy exclusiveness of these south-Dublin suburbs was threatened on a number of occasions from 1880. Dublin Corporation made several attempts to extend the city's boundaries to include the wealthy suburbs of Rathmines and Pembroke. It argued that the high cost of relieving the problems associated with urban poverty—such as a very high death-rate and some of the worst tenement housing in Europe—should be shared by the middle classes who drew their livelihood from the city but opted to live in another tax area. However, the city boundaries were not extended until 1900, when Clontarf and Drumcondra were absorbed into the city. Rathmines and Pembroke, the richest suburbs, were not incorporated into the city until 1930, when, in order to retain their independence, they were forced to make a contribution towards the cost of some city services and they were also required to erect housing for their labouring families. The cottages erected by Pembroke Urban District Council were among the best provided by any Irish local authority. Rathmines again economised, erecting the grim Hollyfield Buildings and Mountpleasant Buildings.

Working class housing

Most labouring and artisan families in Dublin lived in tenements, or to use another word flats. In the early nineteenth century these tenements tended to be in old houses that had been built in the seventeenth or the early eighteenth century, in areas such as the Liberties. As genteel families vacated the large Georgian houses on the north side of the river Liffey, working-class families moved in, leaving these older properties to decay. A one-room tenement in Henrietta Street or Dominick Street often brough a decided improvement in their living conditions, because it offered more space and a structurally-secure building. Some families lived in small cottages, which speculative builders erected, either in the rear of the larger houses, or in the outskirts of the city. Because of the lack of local authority building regulations these cottages were generally over-crowded, squalid, insanitary, and often structurally defective. Families in these cottages lived in worse circumstances than the inhabitants of the better tenements. Most working-class families were forced to tolerate these conditions becaue they could not afford anything better given their low wages and regular periods without work.

Some landlords, notably the Pembroke Estate, built cottages for their workers, just like landlords in rural Ireland. In the industrial towns of England, Scotland and Northern Ireland, some of the first decent working-class houses were provided by large employers. Dublin did not have many large employers, and consequently this type of housing was not common. However, in 1854 the Quaker textile firm, Pim, built cottages for its workers in Harold's Cross, beside their factory and Guinness's brewery erected tenements for its workers in nearby streets. The only other firms to provide a significant number of houses for their workers were the railway companies and the tramway company. Tramway cottages can still be seen in Terenure, Blackrock, Dollymount and Donnybrook. Great Western Square, off the North Circular Road, which was built by the Midland Great Western Company, a development of forty-two houses arranged around a picturesque square, is probably the most attractive of all company housing schemes in the Dublin area. The company built a further forty houses nearby. In all, Dublin employers provided less than 600 houses, a drop in the ocean when we remember that there were over 21,000 families living in one-room tenements in the year of Queen Victoria's death.

By the 1870s some professional and middle-class Dubliners had become concerned that the city's tenements posed a threat to the health and the morals of the city's working-class families. Many tenements were regarded, correctly, as 'fever-nests' and monster stores such as McBirney's and Clery's often sold shirts or suits that were made-up in these 'fever nests', so they posed a real health risk to prosperous citizens. The common staircases found in tenement houses and the doors left open all night were viewed as threatening public morality, while it was believed that over-crowded slums drove working-men to the pub in search of comfort.

The Dublin Artisans' Dwelling Company, which was founded in 1876, was supported by the Earl of Pembroke, the Guinness family, the Earl of Meath, and most of Dublin's top lawyers, doctors and businessmen. It set out to provide decent housing for the city's respectable working families, while earning a return of 5 per cent on the capital invested. This 'five per cent philanthropy' was a feature of English Victorian life at the time: it aimed to combine profit and doing good. Given low or even negative inflation, and the low interest rates at the time, 5 per cent was actually quite a high return on investment. (The yield on Consols, the standard government stock was less than 3 per cent.)

The first scheme carried out by the Dublin Artisans Dwelling Company was a model tenement block in Buckingham Street and the company also intended to renovate and manage other tenement blocks. However, it soon abandoned tenement housing in favour of building cottages, because single-family cottages were regarded as much more respectable and they tended to attract a better class of tenant. In 1880 the company began work on the Coombe scheme, an attractive development of cottages which included squares and other open spaces. However, the company's insistence both on respectability and on earning 5 per cent on its capital meant that the houses were rented by families who were in secure and often well-paid jobs. Many of the inhabitants in the Coombe worked in Guinness's brewery, one of the best employers in the city. Others were army pensioners, who now worked in secure jobs in the government service. The Coombe houses were erected on a site cleared by Dublin Corporation. The previous inhabitants had included many widows who earned meagre sums taking in laundry, doing occasional sewing, or dealing in fruit and vegetables. If there was a male breadwinner, he tended to be a casual labourer or a dealer. None of these former inhabitants moved into the new houses. They were unlikely to have known an investor in the Artisans' Dwelling Company, who might recommend them for a tenancy, tenants were forbidden to clutter the area with vegetable carts, old clothes and scrap or too much laundry, and there was no space to keep a cart or a donkey, and, most importantly, none of the former tenants could have afforded to pay the rents charged.

By the beginning of the twentieth century the Dublin Artisans Dwelling Company had erected over 3,000 houses, mostly on the outskirts of Dublin—Stoneybatter, Infirmary Road, and in Kingstown and Harold's Cross. Their largest development was in Stoneybatter, where all the streets were given names recalling the area's links with Viking Dublin: Olaf Road, Niall Street and Oxmantown Road. The development offered three- and four-roomed cottages and two-storey, five-roomed houses on Oxmantown Road, which were among the best artisans' houses available in the Dublin area. These houses were rented by men in well-paid, secure jobs, often in public service; many were actually in clerical employment. In Oxmantown Road few adult daughters in their late teens or early twenties went out to work, proof that the families were not under financial pressure, and were determined to prove their gentility. These houses are now in great demand especially by young professionals, and are fetching prices that would make their builders and the original occupants stare.

The other major philanthropic housing venture, the Iveagh Trust, which was financed by the Guinness family, also attracted tenants who had secure and respectable jobs. Although the Iveagh Buildings consisted of tenements or apartments, they were extremely roomy and they were finished to a very high standard, both inside and outside. Interestingly, there were few Guinness workers among the tenants; the majority were either skilled artisans employed elsewhere in the city, or public employees, including numerous postmen.

Although Dublin Corporation was not required to show a return of 5 per cent on its houses, it was not authorised by the government to provide housing at a loss, though in practice many of its schemes failed to cover their costs. The Corporation made several attempts to provide cheap and healthy housing for the very poor, but in order to do this, without incurring massive losses, it was forced to erect high-density blocks of tenements that offered very basic facilities. The large development in Corporation Street, which had been previously known as Mabbot Street, in the middle of 'Monto', Dublin's notorious red-light district, was not occupied by the respectable with steady jobs.

However, the new tenement blocks soon came to resemble the older tenements that they were supposed to supplant, and their inhabitants shared the same problems of poverty and poor health. Tenancies in other Corporation schemes tended to be awarded, not on the basis of need, but to families that could afford the rents, which were often double the rents charged in a typical tenement. Most of the families who moved into the Corporation flats in Bride's Alley (directly across from the Iveagh Buildings) had several daughters or sons in their teens and early twenties who were contributing to the family income, and it seems that otherwise they would not have been in a position to meet the rents that were charged. In St Joseph's Place, a small cottage scheme off Dorset Street, which was built on a site which had been cleared of some appalling cottages, none of the former tenants could afford to live in the new houses. There were no criteria at this time for allocating local authority houses, other than ability to pay and perhaps an acquaintance with councillors; so, with the possible exception of Corporation Street, where rents were low because there was little demand for the one-

Strandville Avenue, North Strand

Pembroke Cottages, Ballsbridge

Clonliffe Road, Drumcondra

Lombard Street West, South Circular Road

Builders came up with many solutions to the 'smaller house' problem

room apartments, Corporation houses did not go to those in greatest need.

In 1901, when Queen Victoria died, over 21,000 families in Dublin city were living in one-room tenements, some at densities of five or six per room. Dublin Corporation had provided a mere 1,300 houses and flats. Conditions were, however, probably better than in the 1830s when Victoria came to the throne. Most tenements had running water, but often only via an outdoor tap in the back yard; communal toilets were also in the back yard, many women were reluctant to use them because they were often filthy, and Dublin Corporation made an effort to collect refuse on a regular basis. However, it was not until the 1930s, and indeed really until after the Second World War, that most Dublin working-class families could aspire to a decent home.

The naming of streets

When Catholics began to move to the suburbs in increasing numbers, during the 1870s and 1880s, many of them settled in Drumcondra, partly because it offered cheaper housing than Pembroke or Rathmines (though Harold's Cross would have been an obvious alternative), but also because it offered a more Catholic and less anglicised atmosphere. The delay in developing the north city area meant that there seems to have been little demand for land in Drumcondra until the 1870s, because of the blight caused by the area's slow development. As land was cheap and readily available and the area was close to the city, many Catholic institutions came to the area, notably the seminaries, Holy Cross College Clonliffe and All Hallows College. In the 1860s the foundation stone was laid for the proposed Catholic university at Clonliffe, though it never materialised. Suburban Drumcondra was promoted by men who were nationalists and Catholics. The contrast between the target market for houses in

Drumcondra and the other housing developments sponsored by Lombard and McMahon in the city, and the type of residents that were being attracted to the other suburbs, is immediately apparent if we consider the names that were selected for the new roads, streets and terraces.

Most of the street names selected in Pembroke, Rathmines, Kingstown, Blackrock and Clontarf commemorate the British administration in Ireland, military heroes, the royal family and family names of Anglo-Irish landlords. In both Pembroke and Kingstown numerous roads and terraces were named after the viceroy at the time that they were built: Anglesea, who was appointed in 1828; Northumberland, who succeeded him in 1829; Haddington, who became viceroy in 1834 and Eglinton, appointed in 1852. This was in keeping with past traditions: Dorset Street, Grafton Street and Camden Street were all named after earlier viceroys.

Names associated with the royal family were also popular: Prince of Wales Terrace, Merrion Road; Prince Edward Terrace, Blackrock; Cambridge Terrace, Rathmines; Albert Road, Glenageary and Victoria Road in Rathgar and Dalkey are merely a small sample. Wellington, Waterloo and Marlborough, all in Pembroke, are tributes to British military might; so, more dubiously, is Raglan, named for the commander of the British forces in the Crimean War. Herbert in Ballsbridge, Sydney in Blackrock and Ballsbridge and Pembroke commemorate family names, as do Longford, Vesey and de Vesci in Monkstown, Carysfort in Blackrock and Dalkey, Proby in Blackrock, Vernon in Clontarf, and Palmerston and Temple in Rathmines. Names such as Grosvenor and Belgrave in Rathmines and Monkstown or Eaton in Monkstown were presumably chosen to recall the exclusive streets and squares of the Duke of Westminster's estate in Belgravia. Brighton and Clifton—these two addresses along the seafront at Monkstown—recall English watering-holes;

whereas Dalkey's Vico and Sorrento suggest more exotic locations. Kenilworth Square, Rathmines recalls the romantic historical novel by Sir Walter Scott. Kingstown's Crosthwaite Park,
Crofton Road and Gresham Terrace commemorate the names
of the men that built them, so, rather surprisingly does
Monkstown's Alma Road, though it is also the name of a battle
in the Crimean War.

On the whole, builders were more likely to immortalise
themselves in the names of rows of cottages, rather than in roads
or terraces of imposing houses. Many of these addresses sub-
scribe to the cultural values of an Anglo-Irish, unionist tradition, though it would be foolish to assume that everybody living at these addresses automatically shared such an outlook. By
contrast, when Lombard and McMahon built houses in the
region of the North Circular Road and Dorset Street they selected names that would have evoked Irish, even nationalist
images, both geographical and historical: Killarney Parade,
Glengariff Parade, Geraldine Street, Goldsmith Street. Similar
names crop up in Drumcondra: Grattan Terrace on Drumcondra
Road, Donegal Terrace on Clonliffe Road, Glendalough Road
in Glasnevin and both areas are conspicuous for the large number
of roads and terraces that are named after saints: Saint Alphonsus,
Saint Anne, Saint Brigid, Saint Clare and Saint Columba, to
name but a few—all in Drumcondra, Saint Benedict, Saint David
and Saint Ignatius, and many more, in the adjoining area of the
north city. Drumcondra and Clontarf were annexed to the city
in 1900, Drumcondra willingly, Clontarf under protest, though
it could not afford to provide its residents with proper services.

House styles

During the long years of Victoria's reign the style of houses
changed. The earliest Victorian houses were built of stone or
Portland cement—the material used in most of the seaside ter-

races in Kingstown and Blackrock—or of brownish stock bricks, as in Waterloo Road. By the 1860s, however, when machine-made red bricks came on the market (there were several brick-works on the outskirts of Dublin, in Clondalkin, Bray, Balbriggan, Mount Argus, and Dolphin's Barn), most of the best houses in Pembroke and Rathmines were constructed in that material. In *Seven Winters: Memories of A Dublin Child-hood*, the novelist, Elizabeth Bowen, who was born in Herbert Place, on the city side of the Grand Canal in 1899, describes the roads of Victorian housing in nearby Pembroke.

> The terrain across the canal from us looked open, com-pared to the city on our side. The houses were lower and either light grey or red. The streets were wider; the sheen of the spaced-out slate roofs seemed to reflect itself on the milky sky in which the bells of the many churches dissolved without a fissure of city echo . . . in the 'red roads', such as Raglan Road around Saint Bartholomew's Church an expensive shadowy heaviness, and with it a sort of secrecy, increased. The large plum-red brick houses, with their porches and bow windows and gables, were mansions: they stood apart in lawns behind carriage gates, with evergreen bushes to screen them in. Here trams were quite out of hearing; the residential silence might be taken to be either null or rich. Between the mansions the roads ran almost empty, as though a premium might be set upon walking here.

Houses became brighter and windows become larger. Window tax (which was only levied by Victoria's time on houses with more than six windows) was abolished in 1851, and the duty levied on glass was ended in 1857. Improvements in the tech-nology of glass-making meant that by the 1860s houses could be constructed with large window panes instead of the small leaded windows that were previously favoured. Consequently bay windows became fashionable and more affordable.

In Georgian houses basements, which contained the kitchen and servants' quarters, were generally below ground level. By the middle of the nineteenth century basements tended to be partly or completely above ground. The front door on the first floor was approached by a steep flight of steps. By the 1880s tall three- and four-storey houses, with a full basement and a flight of steps leading to the front door, were no longer fashionable. Terraces now tended to be confined to smaller, cheaper houses; larger houses were detached or semi-detached. In the newer houses, such as those in Orwell Park, there were merely two or three steps down into the kitchen, which was situated at the rear, in the return. The front door and main living rooms were now at garden level and the garden surrounding the house was becoming a more important feature of the house. The style was gradually coming to resemble a modern two-storey suburban villa, whether detached or semi-detached. In the earlier two-storey villas the main reception room and the front door were on the top floor. The transition in style is probably most evident in the houses built on the Palmerston-Temple estate in Rathmines, from the high-Victorian terraced houses erected on Palmerston Road and Palmerston Park in the 1860s to the Cowper Garden houses that were erected by William Pickering in the early twentieth century.

Gardens do not seem to have assumed great importance in the early Victorian houses. The narrow rear gardens of the older terraced houses were often in permanent shadow, and could only be reached via the kitchen quarters. They were probably intended simply as a place to dry clothes, or as a route for removing rubbish and household waste. In larger houses there was a mews, i.e. a stable, at the bottom of the garden with accommodation for a man-servant; the stench of horse would also have discouraged people from using the garden. In the days before water closets became the norm, most houses had an 'ash-pit' at the bottom of the garden that was emptied at regular intervals by a rear lane. The introduction of main sewerage and water-closets and the end of these ash-pits must have helped to make rear gardens more attractive places. Moving the hall door and the main reception rooms to ground level meant that the garden became more accessible and more integrated with the main living rooms. As private gardens assumed greater importance, the practice of providing communal pleasure gardens for the residents, such as those in Kenilworth Square, Rathmines, Crosthwaite Park, Kingstown or Belgrave Squares in Rathmines and Monkstown disappeared.

By the beginning of the twentieth century Ebenezer Howard's concept of a garden city was coming into vogue, and there was an emphasis on lower housing densities and on more open aspects. On the eve of the First World War the new houses at Herbert Park, Cowper Gardens and Foxrock were regarded as the ideal homes. Golf was becoming a popular sport for the Irish middle class. When William Pickering advertised new houses in Cowper Gardens, Rathmines in 1907, he specifically mentioned the 'new Golf links nearby' (Milltown Golf Course); in the 1860s he would have been more likely to mention a new church. Golf, the motor car and the aspiration to live in a more rural environment encouraged the rich to move to Foxrock, Shankhill or to the Burnaby Estate in Greystones.

By the 1920s other factors had combined to make the older Victorian houses appear less attractive. As a consequence of the First World War and the foundation of the Irish Free State, there was a sharp decline in the Protestant population throughout Ireland, and this decline was most marked in the Dublin suburbs. Wartime inflation and the introduction of higher personal tax rates meant that many people who were living on pensions, annuities or investments suffered a severe loss in their incomes and were no longer in a position to keep servants or to live in a large house.

Although the population of Dublin city and suburbs grew rapidly during the 1920s and 1930s, the older Victorian houses did not prosper. Lack of damp-proofing (which only became common just before the First World War), meant that the houses felt cold and damp. Basement kitchens, which had been designed to keep the servants out of sight, did not appeal to modern housewives who did not have the option of sitting upstairs and giving orders to servants. It was tiresome to have to run up and down the stairs to answer the front door-bell or to carry food to the dining table. Housewives wanted a small kitchen adjoining the dining-room. Although many middle-class Irish households continued to keep a live-in servant, because alternative occupations for women were not plentiful, the two-servant household, which had been the norm before 1900, became uncommon.

Modernity was fashionable, period residences were not. The elaborate Victorian houses, complete with plaster mouldings, appeared incompatible with the simpler styles favoured by modern interior design and widely advertised in popular magazines. The 1930s trumpeted Mount Merrion (land which also belonged to the Pembroke Estate) as the ideal address. The Electricity Supply Board presented a luxurious show-house there, complete with an all-electric kitchen and a modern bathroom with hot water on tap. Although it was not impossible to install electric gadgets and modern bathrooms in the older houses, it was costly, and the result seemed less appealing.

Other critical factors also favoured new homes. People were more likely to own their homes from the 1920s onwards. There are several reasons for this. During the First World War, the British government introduced a Rent Restrictions Act, freezing house rents in Britain and Ireland at their existing levels. Although this was an emergency measure introduced during wartime, in an effort to reduce the pressure for higher wages, it proved impossible to repeal the Rent Restrictions Act. Irish farmers had been granted 'fair rents', i.e. rent control, on their land in 1881. Urban tenants demanded similar treatment from the new Irish government and consequently the rent restrictions that were first introduced in 1915 were extended in 1939 and again in 1946. By then they applied to all medium and larger houses built before 1941, though not to furnished bed-sitters.

From the 1920s the policy of the new Irish state favoured home ownership; again this reflected the ethos of rural Ireland where farmers now owned their land, though a similar transition from tenancy to owner-occupancy was also taking place in England. However, most wage and salary earners could only afford to buy a new home. With mortgages from building societies in extremely short supply, most mortgages were provided by local authorities, under the Small Dwellings Acquisition Act; these mortgages were only available for new houses. In addition, from 1924 the government offered subsidies on new homes built for owner-occupiers. Within one or two generations these legislative changes transformed the population of greater Dublin, and urban Ireland in general, from mainly tenant to mainly owner-occupiers. In the process, however, Victorian houses languished in neglect, and areas such as Rathmines and Drumcondra became synonymous with squalid flat-land.

The lack of appreciation shown for Victorian buildings in general did not help their preservation. The rehabilitation of Victorian houses today is due to several factors: greater wealth, more readily available home finance for house purchase, and modern technology. Central heating makes the houses much more habitable in an age when servants are not available to re-plenish fires; modern damp proofing has rehabilitated many basements and the ravages of dry rot and leaking roofs can be repelled. There is a greater appreciation of Ireland's Victorian heritage, and the older suspicion that attached to houses that were strongly associated with the Anglo-Irish has also receded.

With streets full of horses, cattle and other large animals, not always under full control, such railings as these served practical as well as decorative functions. (Barry Mason)

Stained glass was a favourite decoration (Peter Pearson)

The Victorian door is recognisable by its recessed panels and solid mouldings. (Barry Mason)

Typically ornate window surrounds (Peter pearson)

How Victorian
families lived

Mona Hearn

*A young woman reading
in a typically cluttered
interior in the mid-1860s.*

The home had, for the Victorian middle class, an importance far beyond its primary purpose of providing shelter. It represented them, and what they stood for, to the outside world. Home, for many, was one of these suburban houses built, by and large, for the newly emerging middle classes.

The Irish middle class, though small at the beginning of the nineteenth century, grew rapidly in response to the new needs and new opportunities of industrially supplied markets. The result was the emergence of a segment of the population, different from the Ascendancy above them and the working class below, and powerful enough to establish its own unique identity. These people had the economic resources and the freedom to exercise some real choice over how and where they lived. Consequently, the home gained a position of central importance in the lives of the new class.

As we have seen. most of those who led the way into the new suburbs were Protestants. Positions in the public service, the professions, banking, and business were held by Protestants to a far greater extent than their number warranted. In 1871, Catholics had less than half of what could be considered their entitlement of positions in law, medicine and banking, while Protestants, numerically, had more than three times their due share. They were the people who could afford to live in the suburbs; perhaps they were also alienated by the growth of nationalism in the city, and wanted to reside in more homogeneous surroundings among their own kind.

The coming of Victoria to the British throne brought a resurgence in national pride and confidence, while the Great Exhibition of 1851 ushered in an age of prosperity which lasted until the 1870s and engendered feelings of security and certainty which were to extend to the end of the nineteenth century, and perhaps beyond. The Empire grew larger than it had ever been before, in 1876 the Queen acquired the title of Empress of India; British industry grew, overseas trade increased, and the country became more and more wealthy until, by mid-Victorian times, Britain was the richest country in the world. Ireland benefitted from this mid-Victorian prosperity which had a long-lasting effect on the country. Partly because of the continuously falling population, it ended the century among the fifteen richest nations (per capita) in the world. It also benefited, among other things, from changes in the administration of local government, and the boom in transport and communications. The fact that large sections of the population did not partake in this new golden epoch, did nothing to diminish the belief of the well-off in the rightness of the principle of *laissez-faire* and the concepts of self-help and self-reliance, which underlay their good life.

In homes subscribing to this ethos, a distinctly middle-class family pattern grew up. It had certain well-defined characteristics, based on a set of strongly-held values and beliefs—the belief in male superiority, that wife and children owed absolute obedience to husband and father; the belief that a 'lady' did not work and that her vocation in life was a prudent marriage, the primary purpose of which was the procreation of children. The home was the place in which children would be reared in those principles of honour, duty, industry, thrift and sobriety, which would best promote their own well-being and that of society at large. The home, separated, as it now was, from the work-place, became a haven to which the harassed husband could return for

Shopping in the bustle of Grafton Street (above) was quite a different experience to the languid calm of Blackrock (below). Note how the tram tracks swerve to allow Findlaters' carriage trade to stop immediately outside the door.

solace from the strains and stresses of business life. It offered an environment where all the family could live good Christian lives in comfort and privacy.

Protestant unionists considered themselves British and looked to that country and its government as custodians of their economic, spiritual, and cultural well-being; as well as the arbiter in matters of manners, taste and fashion. Many of them regarded Ireland and England as the same country; to those raised in the unionist tradition, London was the most important city in the world, and Dublin had the status of a provincial town. What is probably not as well appreciated, is the extent to which Irish people accepted the status quo, and adopted English culture and its accompanying values. New levels of decorum and propriety were emerging in public and private life: people in different social classes and of all religious persuasions sought 'respectability', a trend which was endorsed by an increasingly powerful and influential Catholic Church.

Thus those moving to the suburbs, Protestants and Catholics alike, had much in common, they all belonged to the wide spectrum of society, newly-designated, the middle class, and, although Elizabeth Bowen described Roman Catholics as 'the others', 'whose world lay alongside ours but never touched', there is no doubt that they shared many values and ambitions. The extent to which the Catholics, especially those emerging from the lower classes and upward bound, had made what might be termed an English life-style their own, is demonstrated very clearly by Joyce in his short story 'The Dead'.

The Misses Morkan, two elderly, Catholic ladies and their niece, who had followed her aunt's career as a music teacher—'many of her pupils belonged to the better-class families on the Kingstown and Dalkey line', and who 'had the organ in Haddington Road' (the richest of all the Catholic parishes)—were holding their annual dance for their family, friends and pupils. They were terrified that Freddy Malins might arrive 'screwed' and shatter the respectability of this gathering; they were anxious that their nephew, Gabriel Conroy, would arrive in time to handle the potentially embarrassing situation. Gabriel taught in a college, lived with his wife and family in Monkstown and considered himself superior to the others present, 'their grade of culture differed from his', a fact which he did not want to advertise by giving a speech above their heads.

Religion played an important part in the lives of all, Catholics and Protestants alike. Sunday was a day devoted to religious observation, on which churchgoing or chapel-going was regarded both as a spiritual necessity and a social requirement. Many of the values endorsed by the middle classes were also affirmed by the Catholic Church, which was a powerful force preaching the sanctity of marriage and the pre-eminence of the family, as indeed, were all the Christian churches. From mid-century the clericalisation of Irish Catholic society, driven in particular by Paul Cullen (Archbishop of Dublin 1852–78), grew apace, and Catholics of all classes came more under the control of the Church. Katherine Tynan recalled that 'an extraordinary wave of Puritanism passed over the Catholic Church in Ireland' in the late 1860s and 1870s, which principally affected her because her mother censored, very strictly, the novels she was reading.

Father was the undoubted head of the domestic hierarchy, whose word was (at least theoretically) law within the home. Wives were economically dependent on their spouses; they were also used, as women, to playing a subordinate role even within the household and, of course, were not expected to have any knowledge of the big world outside. In *A Portrait of the Artist as a Young Man*, Mr Dedalus is the dominant father personified, as he stands in front of the mantelpiece, under the pierglass, waxed moustache ends curling upwards, coat tails parted, the better to warm his posterior—incidentally depriving the rest of the gathering of the heat of the fire—while he waits for his wife and the servants to serve Christmas dinner.

Being middle-class

Membership of the middle class was never a matter solely of income or occupation, though both of these were important. Values, beliefs, aspirations, tastes—life-style—were also clearly involved. In 1901 the pioneering English writer on social themes, Seebohm Rowntree, made the employment of a servant the distinguishing feature between the middle class and the working class, on the principle that a resident servant promoted a woman into a 'lady'. In Ireland a minimum income of £150 a year was required to afford a servant, yet the middle class could not be categorised by this criterion alone. In Britain, where those with an income of £150–£200 were regarded as just 'scraping in', the difficulty posed by clerks earning only £60–£80 a year, dressing like gentlemen, but scarcely able to live like gentlemen, arose. John Burnett, in A *Social History of Housing,* suggests that membership of the middle class entailed some margin of income over necessary expenditure, a strong sense of respectability, sobriety, polite manners, Christian observance, the ability to keep a wife who did not work outside the home, and a deeply-rooted belief that the family and the home were the pillars both of a good society and of private happiness. Above all, the home, and the house which accommodated it, were of central interest and importance. To choose it, furnish and decorate it, repair and care for it provided satisfaction which was far more than material—a proper place in which to rear children, to entertain friends, to retreat from the cares of the world and take an honest pride in one's possessions and achievements.

The middle class covered a wide spectrum of the population. In fact three social strata can be identified, the lower-middle class, the upper-middle class and, in between, the middle-

middle class, with a degree of overlap, especially between the last two. In 1909 L. C. Money defined the upper-middle class as those earning more then £700, and the middle- and lower-middle class, as earning between £700 and £160 (the point at which income tax then began), without defining a monetary boundary between the last two. Initially, housing in the new suburbs was provided for those from the middle to the upper end of the scale, but from the mid-1870s houses were built for those with much more modest incomes.

From the 1901 Census, for instance, we learn that the residents of Temple Road, Rathmines, were at the upper end of the social scale. Five were members of the higher professions, six were proprietors of large businesses, such as George Jacob, the biscuit manufacturer, and five widows and two single ladies had independent means. All the households employed servants, with eleven having two, two houses having three, and three households, four; two employed a male servant, which was considered a status symbol. Louie Bennett said of Temple Road in the 1880s, it 'was the refuge of highly respectable business people, anxious to escape from the social zone allotted to the world of trade and commerce', and, of the people, 'we wore good manners all the time'.

The residents of Clyde Road, Pembroke, in 1901 were somewhat similar to those in Temple Road. Independent means such as annuities and interest from property, are, of course, impossible to access; however, the location and rateable valuation of the house, the keeping of servants, the occupations of other members of the family, all indicated a comfortable style of living. All households employed servants, ninety per cent having two or more. The earnings of the householders are impossible to gauge, but at least £1,000 a year was needed to keep four servants. Many would have earned much more; judges earned £3,500, senior civil servants got £2,000, senior fellows in Trinity College,

Tennis on the lawn of a newly-built house in Temple Road, Rathmines

*A rather formally dressed family group, unusually posed with their
servant, at the turn of the century*

£1,300–£1,600, a small number of the very top barristers could earn as much as £5,000 a year, but the average was £800–£1,000.

In roads such as St Mary's Road, Pembroke, Castle Avenue, Clontarf, and Belgrave Square, Rathmines, the rateable valuation was £30–£40 as against £60–£70 in Clyde Road, and rents were £40–£50 per annum compared with £80–£120 in the more exclusive areas. Here there was a much wider range of occupations. A very large proportion, forty per cent, virtually all women, lived on annuities, fourteen per cent were members of the higher professions, eleven per cent belonged to the lower professions, such as teachers, twelve per cent were merchants. Eighty-six per cent of households on these roads employed servants, fifty four per cent having one servant; two houses in Belgrave Square even had a male servant.

Heads of households in Oxford Road, Ranelagh, included seven skilled men and women and three male clerks; five lived on annuities (four of them women), and four women lived on income from boarders and lodgers; other occupations represented in the twenty-four houses were shop assistants and a commercial traveller. Carlingford Road, in Drumcondra, catered for similar tenants. Two households in Oxford Road kept a general servant, no household on Carlingford Road employed a servant. The vast majority of the Carlingford and Oxford Road householders earned less than the £150 required to keep a resident servant, though many would have employed the services of a charwoman. Skilled men earned about £100 a year, post-office clerks slightly more, and while shop assistants' wages varied greatly, a range from £40 to £75 was usual.

Virtually all the suburbs had a substantially greater proportion of Protestant residents than the city. Heads of households in sixty-eight per cent of all houses on these suburban roads belonged to the Church of Ireland, or churches other than the Catholic Church. At the top of the social scale, in Clyde Road and Temple Road, only one-sixth of the residents were Catholic.

Enough to marry on?

Guidance on every aspect of daily living was generously supplied by books (of which Mrs Beeton's *Household Management* is only the most famous) and also by columns devoted to household affairs in weekly and monthly publications. The authors—who were invariably women—wrote in an authoritative, even didactic manner. They prescribed how the lady of the house was to cope with her new responsibilities, from acquiring, furnishing, and equipping a house, to hiring and managing a servant, planning meals, buying food and clothing, bringing up children and entertaining guests.

Most English writers agreed that the appropriate fraction of income to be devoted to house rent was about one-tenth, and normally should not exceed one-eighth; this should include rates and taxes. The fraction suggested by Irish writers was larger, one-eighth, and it would seem likely that this represented reality. Whereas in Britain the rent of a house was usually set at one-twentieth of the cost, in Ireland it was nearer to one-tenth of the cost, which made investment in property profitable, and rents high. Thus in 1880, four houses in Bloomfield Avenue could be bought for £1,500 (i.e. £375 each), which were let for £36, £38, £40, £40 (advertisement in *The Irish Times*, 3 January 1880). In 1904, a house on Kenilworth Square could be purchased for £630 or rented for £60 (*The Irish Times* 4 January).

Young people were also advised to 'spare as much of their income as possible' to rent a good house. 'Your success in life is often influenced by the neighbourhood in which you live, and no house can be considered cheap that is in a second-rate locality.' (This was from Findlater's *Ladies' Housekeeping Book* for 1896.) A middle-class man could hardly afford to get married before the age of thirty. He needed an income of at least £250—

£300 before he could live in conditions that might be acceptable to a new wife, not to mention a father-in-law. Even in Carlingford Road, where rents would have been comparatively low, there were only four heads of household in the twenty-five to thirty age group; three of these were married, without children, one kept three boarders, who would have supplemented income. In Belgrave Square there was a coachman, married with one young daughter, and an insurance official, married, with no family, who kept two boarders. All the other heads in the roads sampled were over thirty. Female heads of household, thirty-one per cent of the sample, were over forty, with the exception of two widows in their thirties. Women, as they did not earn their own livelihood, had to wait until parents or husbands died

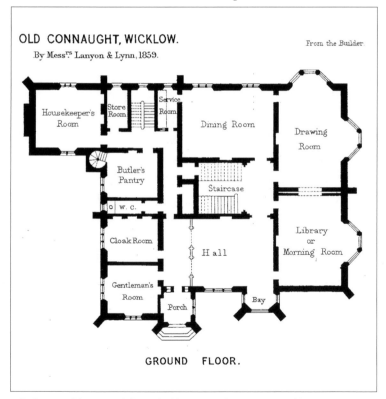

The layout of the ground floor of Old Connaught, a very grand house in Wicklow—note the amount of space allocated to the butler and the housekeeper

before assuming that position.

A young man marrying on £300 a year, employing one servant, and hoping to start a family, would have found it necessary
to budget very carefully. Food would have accounted for at least
thirty per cent of income; clothing, seventeen per cent; rent twelve
and a half per cent; fuel four and a half per cent, eight per cent
for servant (£9 for wages and £16 for keep); eight per cent for
savings; four per cent, taxes, rates; health, four per cent; travelling to work or shopping, four per cent; recreation, five per
cent: this leaves three per cent for small household expenses. He
would have required three to four bedrooms, for himself and
his wife, children, and servant, two reception rooms, kitchen
and scullery—a six or seven-roomed house.

Later, as his career developed, the number of children increased, or a second servant was hired, he and his family might
move to a larger more expensive house, with a more imposing
hall, finer reception rooms and an extra bedroom. Finally, between the ages of forty-five and fifty, he might be able to move
to a house of character on a fashionable road with ten rooms—
spacious hall, large dining-room, elegant drawing-room, study,
kitchen and ancillary rooms and six bedrooms. This was deemed
adequate to house his teenage or grown family, visitors, three or
four servants, and to live and entertain in a manner appropriate
to his enhanced position. Heads of households were generally
in their fifties before they could afford to live in the more expensive areas of Dublin city. In 1901, slightly less than one quar-
ter of those living in Temple Road, and only thirty per cent of
the residents of Clyde Road, were under fifty. In the sixty-four
houses of Belgrave Square, only eleven per cent of heads were
under forty. Those renting houses on roads such as Oxford and
Carlingford might have been happy to be regarded as respectable people living in a quiet, genteel neighbourhood; their incomes, derived from annuities, and such occupations as skilled

A peaceful afternoon in Ranelagh

work, clerk, shop assistant, boarding-house keeper, did not allow much scope for career development.

Contemporary advice was not to take a lease longer than three years, since by then changing income and family needs would encourage a move to a better suited house. People moved house frequently; perhaps the fact that they only rented meant they had no lasting attachment to a particular house. A tenant would not be inclined to put up with inconveniences that a house-owner must endure or pay to have corrected. This led to a surprising mobility. Thus there was a fifty-nine per cent turnover in house occupancy in St Mary's Road, Pembroke, between 1891 and 1896, and a forty-six per cent turnover between then and 1901. In Clyde Road, the turnover was forty-three per cent between 1891 and 1896, and thirty-nine per cent between 1896 and 1901. In Temple Road, Rathmines, an area of very expensive houses, the turnover was fifty per cent between 1891 and 1896, and a modest twenty-six per cent between 1896 and 1901. (These figures are based on *Thom's* annual post office directories, and can be relied on; postmen were paid a bonus for reporting changes of occupancy.) In *Portrait of the Artist,* James Joyce, who came from a family of inveterate house-movers, describes the 'two great yellow caravans' used in one of these moves, and how he and his mother saw them, from the window of the railway carriage, as they lumbered heavily along the Merrion Road bound for their new address. It must have been a common sight in Dublin from the 1850s until well into the new century.

A middle-class man, earning £400–£500, with a young family and one or two servants, willing to spend one-eighth of his income, or somewhat more, on accommodation, could rent a suitable house in the township of Rathmines for around £40–£50. In 1880 a house on Charleston Road, Rathmines could be rented for £45 per annum, while a house in 'the best part of Rathgar'—as the advertisement in *The Irish Times* (3 January 1880) put it—for which the previous tenant had paid £50 was on offer for forty guineas. The cost of living, and presumably rents, had decreased from the 1850s by about eight per cent. In 1904 a good house in Rathmines, containing seven or eight apartments, could be rented for between £40 and £50. A five-roomed house on Leinster Place cost £28, and a seven-apartment house in Fairview, £36. Of course, rent depended, not only on the size of house, but on its location. The rent of a nice cottage near the harbour in Dalkey was £40. A 'splendid house' at 9 Newbridge Avenue, adjoining Lansdowne Road, was offered for £60. A house on Raglan Road, Pembroke, could be bought for £1,500 or rented for £120 per annum. It had four reception rooms, five bedrooms, bathroom, servants' accommodation, garden and stabling.

Furniture and decorating

Once established in their new homes, the Victorians believed in buying good quality furniture which would last their lifetime and probably that of their children as well. Young housewives were urged to buy furniture by degrees and with great care and deliberation. Findlater's *Ladies Housekeeping Book* urged them to avoid 'suites of cheap furniture', and to attend auctions in 'respectable houses' where they could 'pick up first-class pieces at moderate prices'. They should spend as much as they could afford on carpets—Wilton or Axminster would, if properly cared for, last a lifetime. Strip carpet was used on the stairs, held in place with stair rods made from polished wood or brass. It could be shifted up or down a few inches, some advocated every two months, to spread wear and tear; it could also be lifted easily for cleaning. Carpet squares or large rugs on parquet flooring were much more common than fitted carpets. These could be lifted easily for cleaning, or when moving house. The wooden surround was stained and polished; sometimes the whole floor was stained and the carpets rolled up, cleaned and laid aside for a rest during the summer months.

A clear demarcation had evolved distinguishing public rooms, family rooms and rooms for the servants. Smaller houses had a parlour, or drawing-room, and dining-room; larger houses, parlour, dining-room and drawing-room, which might be on the first floor, and extend over the parlour and hall below. These were the public rooms. The best reception room was the drawing-room, where furnishings expressed the taste and wealth of the family. Important guests were received in this room. Grander homes may also have had a study for the master, and a morning-room, where the lady of the house received visitors in the

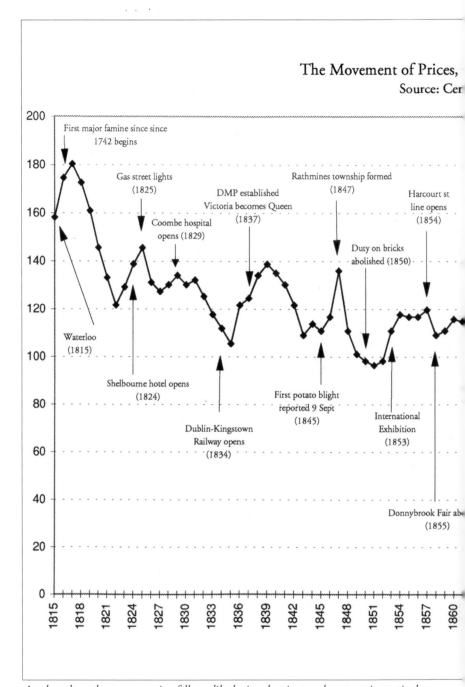

As a broad trend, consumer prices fell steadily during the nineteenth century, in particular between 1875 and 1895.

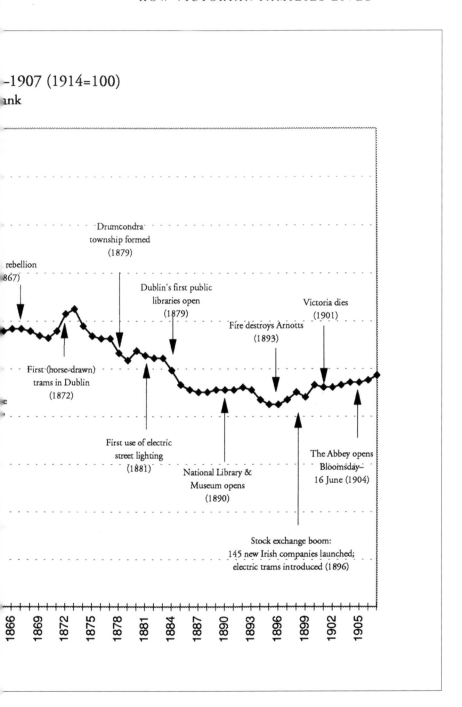

–1907 (1914=100)

ank

rebellion
867)

Drumcondra
township formed
(1879)

Dublin's first public
libraries open
(1879)

Victoria dies
(1901)

Fire destroys Arnotts
(1893)

First (horse-drawn)
trams in Dublin
(1872)

First use of electric
street lighting
(1881)

National Library &
Museum opens
(1890)

The Abbey opens
Bloomsday
16 June (1904)

Stock exchange boom:
145 new Irish companies launched;
electric trams introduced (1896)

1866 1869 1872 1875 1878 1881 1884 1887 1890 1893 1896 1899 1902 1905

morning, interviewed servants and did her household accounts. Once inside the door (painted 'crimson, chocolate, chestnut, ink-blue or olive-green' as Elizabeth Bowen remembered, with the occasional dashing chalk-white), the hall was not just a passageway, it proclaimed the status of the family and the comfort in which they lived. It, the stairway, public rooms and family bedrooms were usually wallpapered.

Fashion preferred rooms to be filled to overflowing with large, heavy furniture, and this was clearly reflected in the reception rooms, most displaying an eclectic mixture of styles. Heavily-upholstered chairs, which might include the quaintly named 'indulging chair', and settees were deep-buttoned, often upholstered in rich ruby velvet, perhaps with matching red rep curtains. Sometimes curtains and pelmet were patterned with bright, multi-coloured garlands of flowers, again matching the upholstered furniture. Anti-macassars were put on the backs of chairs, to protect them from the macassar oil used to keep hair in place. Lighter curtains close to the glass were usually of Nottingham lace, which ensured privacy and protected the carpet and upholstery from fading. In the grander drawing-rooms, artificial light might be provided by a six-light crystal gasolier. Numerous pictures were suspended from picture rails (introduced in the 1880s), oils were preferred for the dining-room, watercolours and tapestries for the parlour and drawing-room. Small tables with sewing boxes, often made of papier-mâché inlaid with mother-of-pearl, which was very popular, were placed conveniently around the room.

Many parlours and drawing-rooms had a what-not, which was a tiered stand, on which a palm or other potted plant and a plethora of small ornaments could be displayed. Other treasures could be shown off in a glass-shelved display cabinet, or the so-called 'specimen' table. The round mahogany pedestal table was covered with a patterned fringed cloth, while a couple of balloon-backed chairs with cabriole legs stood nearby. An important piece of furniture in most homes was the piano; it was essential for the female members of the family who were taking music lessons, and was indispensable for musical evenings. Birds of paradise, stuffed and mounted under a glass dome, or shell ornaments also under glass domes, were common. A pair of fire screens, to shield the ladies' make-up from the heat of the fire, were placed at either side of the chimney-breast. The fire-grate was cast iron, usually with a white marble surround, and often, a large overmantel mirror with gilt frame reflected the grandeur of the room. If the house had a drawing-room and parlour, the former was reserved for entertaining and special occasions, and the parlour was used every day by the family. The dining-room was reserved for dining and for family prayers.

A neo-Celtic style of art, reviving forms and motifs from early Irish art, began to emerge about the 1840s. The impact was seen initially in metalwork and later in woodwork. Articles of furniture, including chairs, settles and cabinets, were carved or painted with interlaced patterns. In the late nineteenth century the Arts and Crafts movement, which was interested in handicrafts and design, gave neo-Celticism a new boost, and was responsible for the introduction of some elegant furniture into the Dublin Victorian home.

In her memoirs *Myself and Others,* the novelist Annie M. P. Smithson (who was born in 1873) described her grandparents' home at 42 Claremont Road, Sandymount. It was not large, but a comfortable, middle-class Victorian house. It had a small garden, gay with flowers in spring and summer. The hall was pleasant, with a long table down one side, on which stood pots of plants and a little fancy tray for visitors' cards. Facing the door was a big grandfather clock. The drawing-room was to the left with green Venetian blinds, and lace curtains in summer and heavy ones in winter. The carpet was a vivid green with

The High Victorian fireplace, complete with two tier over-mantel, patterned tassled fringe on the mantelpiece, and even curtains (1891)

(above) The drawing-room of a house in Lindsay Road, Drumcondra, photographed a few years later, was only a little less elaborate. (below) The Lindsay Road house from the outside—blinds and lace curtains in every window, and bicycles in the neighbour's front garden

clusters of big pink roses. Opposite the door, on a marble-topped table, was an image of Ganesh, the Elephant God, under a glass dome, which her grandfather had brought home from a trip around the world. This was the terror of Annie's childhood. Beside this room was the dining-room, which was more homely and which she liked better. It had a big sideboard on which stood the silver teapot and kettle, cake and fruit dishes 'seldom empty'. There was the usual bell rope to call the servants. There were prints on the wall of biblical themes, and of loyal British subjects, one, the Duke of Wellington. The big comfortable kitchen, where she remembers the cook basting a joint as it turned slowly on the spit, was down a short passage near the back door to the garden The house had four family bedrooms, as well as the servant's bedroom. Her grandmother slept in a large canopied bed with curtains; at a time when most bed-rooms were unheated, hangings protected against draughts, and kept the sleeper cosy and warm.

In contrast to the 'typical' Victorian room, the drawing room of Elizabeth Bowen's childhood (she was born in 1899) had 'a doubly watery character from being green in tone'. The walls were covered with light green moiré wallpaper. Florentine mir-rors 'wreathed in spiked gilt leaves', and sketches in gilt frames, replaced the much more common heavily framed oil paintings and tapestries displayed on floral walls. The chesterfield sofa and armchairs were covered in pink and cream 'shadow' cretonne. 'Lightness was given by frilled white muslin inner curtains, and the frilled white muslin slips (embroidered with harps and sham-rocks) over the pink cushions'. Her mother's carved cherry-wood writing table was in the light of one of the windows. Of course, at that time, Victorian taste was already giving way to the sim-pler styles favoured by the Edwardians.

Water, heat and light

Many changes occurred between the 1850s and the close of the century which improved the quality of life for the middle classes. One of the most important, especially for housewives and servants, were advances made in water supply and sanitation. Until the mid-1880s Rathmines residents were supplied with canal water of a very dubious quality, since the township refused to take water from the Vartry scheme which was already supplying water to the Pembroke township as well as Dublin city as this would increase the rates. The situation was finally improved when Rathmines developed its own waterworks at Bohernabreena, taking water from the Dodder.

For the disposal of human refuse, a privy at the rear of the house, or the bottom of the garden, was used. An unpopular part of the housemaids' work was the emptying of all the chamber-pots used during the night into this cesspit. A simple cesspool required frequent emptying by the so-called 'night-soil' men who came and went by a back entrance, not through the front of the house (hence the network of little lanes behind some of the older Victorian streets). Drains were originally designed for the removal of surface water. It was only after the Public Health Act, 1878, that water closets were regularly introduced into houses in Dublin city, and privies and cesspools were done away with under the administration of the Chief Medical Officer, Sir Charles Cameron.

External plumbing was introduced in England after the Prince of Wales's typhoid attack in 1871, soil and waste-pipes being placed on the outside walls of the houses, with free ventilation and intercepting traps. This allowed water-closets to be brought indoors. The WC began to be included as an integral part of a new English house in the 1860s and 1870s usually on the main bedroom floor, with another on the ground floor, near the kitchen quarters, for servants. Until the 1860s, running water was rarely piped beyond the kitchen, and that was only a cold supply. People bathed in a tin bath before the kitchen fire; the better-off used a hip or lounge bath in front of their bedroom fire. In all cases the baths had to filled and emptied by hand, and the hot water heated by the kitchen range.

In Dublin progress would seem to have been slower than in England. Advertisements for suburban housing in 1860 did not mention water-closets or baths. In January 1880 a 'desirable' house in the neighbourhood of Rathgar was required to rent or purchase at £500–£1,000. It had to be well-built, and have four to five bedrooms and sewage. A house on Charleston Road., Rathmines, had gas, pipe water, garden front and rear; bathroom or WC were not mentioned. Most advertising, even for 'superior ' housing did not say that there was bathroom or indoor sanitation.

Prior to 1881, when the combined townships of Pembroke and Rathmines introduced a new drainage system, the sewage from Rathmines, and a considerable portion from the higher level of Pembroke Township, was discharged by the 'Swan' sewer, into the river Dodder. This polluted the banks of the Liffey, and was taken by the flood into the heart of Dublin. Sewage from the low lying portion of Pembroke stagnated in ditches or was carried by these ditches to the Blackrock township, and discharged on to the strand. The results in both instances, were very objectionable. The new system discharged raw sewage into the estuary of the Liffey beyond low water mark. This was in its turn criticised, especially when Dublin Corporation introduced its new main drainage scheme in 1906, which, in contrast to the Pembroke/Rathmines scheme, incorporated sewage treatment works, the sludge being discharged outside the port and bay of Dublin, not less than six miles from Poolbeg Lighthouse.

In fact many of the houses in the 'best' parts of the suburbs did not get indoor sanitation and bathrooms until the 1890s.

Thus in July 1891 the sanitation firm of Fletcher and Phillipson, laid down drains 'in the new', at 7 Palmerston Villas, which had been built in the 1850s; at 22 Leeson Park, the next month; at 1 Clyde Road in November 1892; at 11 Waterloo Place, in November 1893. In 1892, 11–14 and 16 Charleville Road had WCs installed near the kitchen, sinks with running water in the sculleries, and WCs and perhaps bathrooms put in upstairs. Roebuck House, Clonskeagh, had all old foul water drains destroyed and new ones installed, in February 1891.

The house was heated by coal fires, and cooking was done on an open fire or coal range. By the 1850s iron ranges were readily available. Open ranges were the first improvement on open hearths—a basket grate was set between an oven and a water tank. Boiling was done on top, and roasting on a spit in front of the fire. Closed ranges, which had a small fire behind iron doors, hot-water tank and hotplates, and flues to guide the heat around the oven, were the next improvement. The heat was easier to control by means of dampers, food was less likely to have a 'smoky' taste, and pots and pans were easier to clean. The kitchen range had to be set and lit very early in the morning to heat water for washing and shaving, and to cook the breakfast.

Lighting was provided by candles and oil-lamps, and the first person up on dark mornings had to find her way downstairs to the cold kitchen by means of the flickering light of a candle. The range and open fires in living-rooms required constant attention during the day. Coal scuttles and buckets were filled with coal from basement coal cellars, into which the coal was delivered through an outside opening, or, in smaller houses, from a shed in the back yard. It was reckoned that a middle-class household used at least a ton of coal a month: if there was a fire in the nursery or parlour, more was required.

Oil-lamps were trimmed and refilled with oil every day. Gas was first used to light the streets of Dublin on 5 October 1825, and its use was gradually adopted for lighting private houses.

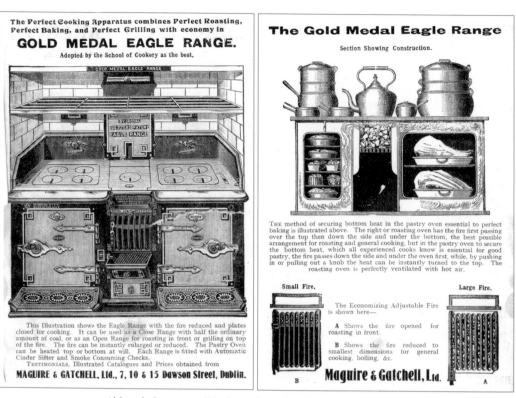

Although the range still had to be lit and tended as a fire, it gave cooks much greater control

The introduction of gas lighting into the home saved the trouble of filling and trimming oil lamps, but it was only with the coming of the incandescent mantle, after 1884, that a good gas light was obtained. Gas lighting was generally only installed in the hall and reception rooms, lamps and candles being used in the rest of the house. Indeed many households continued to use these methods until electric lighting became available. In 1892 Dublin Corporation first supplied street lighting and offered current to citizens who wished to install electric lighting in their own homes. This offer was taken up very slowly by householders; in 1904 there were only 650 consumers in Dublin and most of those were only using it for lighting or as power for industry.

Domestic toil

There was an immense amount of work involved in keeping the family members comfortably housed, warm, well-fed and clean. In households without domestic help, this task devolved on the wife; in houses with servants, the work was shared, but the larger houses and the more elaborate life style meant that the undertaking was not any easier. There were virtually no machines in the home and everything had to be done laboriously by hand, often under very difficult circumstances.

Writers on household management had plenty of advice to offer young housekeepers of the upper and middle classes on the organisation of the housework and the management of servants. The importance of good organisation was stressed, for, as *Findlater's Ladies Housekeeping Book* admonished, no husband liked coming home to find his wife 'with a dull complexion, leaden eyes, a bad headache, and a worse temper'; a beautiful, neat, shining, dust-free house did not compensate, they were told. They were urged to employ efficient servants, as these, after the judicious mistress, were of most importance to the comfort and regularity of the household.

To achieve a well-organised home, and to use servants efficiently, it was advised that the daily work, and weekly or fortnightly tasks, should be planned, written down clearly on a strong card, and given to each servant. Mrs Humphrey, otherwise known as 'Madge' of the magazine *Truth,* suggested the following daily chores for a housemaid, in a family of four, with a cook and a maid:

6.30—Open windows in drawing-room; sweep and dust that room and stairs

7.00—Take bath-water to bedrooms, and call everybody (fires had to be lighted and water boiled before this could be done)

7.15—Lay breakfast table

7.45—Dining-room breakfast and kitchen breakfast

8.30—Go to bedrooms, open windows, turn down beds; empty basins and chamber-pots

9.00—Make the beds, dust the rooms, and afterwards do special work of day

1.00—Be dressed for afternoon, and lay luncheon table. (It was usual, when only two servants were employed, for the house-maid to dress in a cotton print dress, large white apron and cap in the morning, and in parlourmaid's attire, of black dress, small fancy apron, and hair band, when waiting on table and answering the door in the afternoon. In many houses she was called a house-parlourmaid.)

The afternoon programme was:

1.30—Luncheon and kitchen dinner

2.15—Clear away lunch, and wash glasses and silver

4.30—Kitchen tea

5.00—Drawing-room tea

7.00—Lay dining-room table

7.30—Wait at dinner

8.30—Wash up glasses and silver, dessert plates, ice plates, and finger glasses

9.00—Kitchen supper

10.0—Bedtime.

The Victorian house was difficult to keep clean as fires, candles, and oil-lamps deposited a film of soot on everything in the house. This was added to in the summer by dust from the roads and streets; in winter mud from the roads was carried in on shoes, in spite of the iron boot-scrapers found outside the front door of many houses. The task was not made any easier by the Victorians' tendency to fill their homes with large quantities of furniture, pictures and ornaments. Elaborate plasterwork, mouldings, ledges, panels and cluttered rooms made the cleaner's job an unenviable one. In addition work methods, such as using feather dusters and sweeping carpets with a whisk, even if the carpet was spread, as advised, with damp tea leaves, merely displaced much of the dust.

Special tasks were spread over a two-week period, and ensured that all rooms in the house, stairs and hallways, were cleaned thoroughly within that period; plate and brasses were also polished. Thorough cleaning required 'turning out' a room, and this was not an easy task. Pictures and mirrors and ornaments were removed and cleaned. Furniture was moved to the centre of the room and covered with dust sheets. Ceilings and walls were swept down with a long-handled brush. Windows were washed and polished, the mantlepiece and grates thoroughly cleaned. Plenty of tea leaves were spread and the carpet 'twigged', the stained surround was beeswaxed, furniture polished, and everything replaced. By keeping the whole house clean from day to day, the 'abomination known as spring cleaning', the housewife was assured, could be reduced to washing paint and lifting carpets.

The joys of cooking

In a small household it was the cook's job to prepare all meals for family and staff, as well as for dinner parties and special occasions. She might also answer the door in the mornings, clean the kitchen scullery, downstairs hall and kitchen stairs and help the housemaid with the thorough cleaning of drawing-room and dining-room. She might also be expected to wash woollens and iron. The mistress was advised, however, that servants could not 'go on working all day', and that it was wise to arrange a little 'off-time' for them in the afternoons, when they could darn their stockings, mend their clothes, write letters, 'or otherwise amuse themselves in their own way'. This leisure time should be spent in the kitchen and they should be dressed and tidy before settling down to enjoy themselves.

The storage, preparation and cooking of food all presented

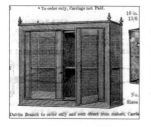

Meat safes, from the catalogue of the Junior Army and Navy Store, D'Olier Street

problems for the housewife. Milk, meat, fish and perishable foods were, if possible, bought daily, as the storage of these items was extremely difficult. The vast majority of the middle classes had a meat larder where the meat and fish were stored on a slate shelf, under fine wire covers, to keep the flies away. Some of the smaller houses might only have had a meat safe hanging on the wall outside the back door. Housewives were advised to examine meat every day, to scrape off the outside if there was the least appearance of mould on mutton, beef or venison and to flour the part. Peppering meat helped to keep flies off, or the joint might be saved by wrapping it in a cloth and burying it overnight in a hole dug in fresh earth.

Meat arrived unprepared or crudely prepared, and had to be cut up, boned, trimmed and made ready for the oven or spit. Fowl, and game had to be plucked, cleaned out and trussed. Fish required cleaning, and, if not cooked whole, filleting or cutting into other suitable pieces. Milk was delivered daily by the milkman, who transferred the required amount with pint or quart measure into the customers' jugs. It was not, of course, pasteurised. Butter, bought by the pound, was formed into fancy balls using butter hands, before being served at table. Vegetables and fruits could only be bought in season, so bottling and preserving were necessary skills for the cook to acquire. Bread-making was an important part of the work in most kitchens.

Cooking conditions were also difficult. Food was prepared on plain wooden tables which had to be scrubbed frequently. Wood ash was used to scour iron and copper kitchen utensils. Knives, which were made of steel, had to be cleaned with bath brick on a knife board before each meal. The kitchen sink, usually located in the scullery, was made of stone, though later glazed earthenware was used. While cold water was available at the scullery sink, or from a tap in the yard, hot water was heated on open fires or the range and carried to the sink in large heavy pots

Decorative brickwork (Barry Mason)

The importance of fire in the domestic economy made chimneys a key architectural feature (Barry Mason)

or kettles. If a draining board was fitted, it was made of wood and required careful scouring to keep it free of dirt and slime. The range had to be carefully 'managed' to maintain the correct temperature for the cooking process required. Cooking on an open fire was much more difficult, and necessitated cleaning sooty pots, and an even more heavily smoke-begrimed kitchen. To add to the problem, the more prosperous members of the middle class ate very large meals consisting of a number of courses, many of elaborately prepared dishes.

The formal dinner party which might have three or four courses, each with multiple dishes, really taxed the ability of the kitchen staff and the mistress. The frequency with which this occurred depended on individual circumstances, both social and economic; a dinner party might be given monthly. Again Mrs Beeton had advice: the number of guests should never exceed twelve, so that conversation could be general. The order of food was from the most substantial to the lightest, the order of drinking wine, from the mildest to the most foamy and most perfumed. 'To invite a person to your house is to take charge of his happiness so long as he is beneath your roof.'

The middle class drank well. Champagne was the favourite wine. Port, sherry, burgundy, claret and German wines were all popular. Every autumn, Eilis Dillon's grandfather received tiny sample bottles of wine from Bordeaux for tasting. The barrels were then ordered, and a man from a public house came for a day or two to bottle the wine. One year he bought a hundred dozen of good claret which was selling for a shilling a bottle, a bargain even in those days.

During the second half of the century, it was considered smart to include French dishes. In 1873 Morrison's Hotel in Dublin offered its customers French cuisine (*The Weekly News*, Saturday 1 February 1873). It was only in late Victorian times, that it became fashionable for the upper classes to dine out at hotels and restaurants. Formerly only men had eaten out at their clubs and restaurants.

The day-to-day eating style in the family was, of course, much less elaborate. The typical English breakfast of porridge, fish, bacon and eggs, toast and marmalade, came into being in the nineteenth century and was adopted in this country. Previous to that cold meats and cheese were served for breakfast, and in some houses this continued. 'The moral and physical welfare of mankind depends largely on its breakfast', wrote Mrs Beeton in 1861. Her menu for a family dinner on a Sunday in January was: boiled turbot and oyster sauce and potatoes, for the first course. This was followed by roast leg of pork, apple sauce, broccoli and potatoes. The sweet was cabinet pudding and damson tart, made with preserved damsons. On Monday, the remains of the turbot were warmed in the oyster sauce and served with potatoes. The main course was cold pork, but stewed steak was also served, with vegetables. The sweet was open jam tart, which should have been made with the pieces of paste left from the damson tart.

Ordinarily, the upper class and many of the middling class had their main meal of the day in the evening, usually about seven o'clock, when the master came home. The lower-middle class, who often lived in the inner suburbs and could walk home at mid-day, or take a penny tram ride, had their dinner in the middle of the day. Servants and the youngsters in the nursery also dined in the middle of the day ; this freed servants to serve evening dinner, after which they had their last meal of the day, supper, at about nine o'clock. Mothers might join the children at their meal in the nursery and have a light lunch with them.

Cookery books of this time were full of recipes for using up leftovers, trying to avoid leftovers was never mentioned. Housewives were sternly told that the roast leg of tender juicy mutton, 'which is too often our idea of a good wholesome dinner' could be replaced by tasty dishes using leftovers. Bread staled rapidly, so puddings which used up dry bread were very common. For a light lunch, the remains of cold joints, some hashed meat, poultry or game with bread, cheese and biscuits and a few sweets, was served.

The weekly wash

Most household tasks paled into insignificance when compared with the weekly wash. So serious an effort was it that it was commonly cited as a cause of breakdown in women's health. Anyone who could afford to paid a charwoman to come in every Monday or Tuesday to do the washing. The wise mistress made it a condition of employment, before engaging a servant, if she wished her to do the laundry. Many servants, when advertising for a position, stipulated whether they were willing or unwilling to do the washing. Sometimes a washerwoman collected the dirty clothes on a Monday and brought them back clean later in the week. Perhaps surprisingly, commercial laundries did not develop to any great extent in Dublin until the latter part of the nineteenth century. The trade was listed for the first time in *Thom's Directory* in 1865, when three laundry keepers were named.

In a well-run house, clothes were sorted the day before, shirts, collars and cuffs in one bundle, handkerchiefs in another, table linen—cloths, napkins and d'oyleys—bed-linen and towels, body-linen, flannels and woollens, and coloured garments in separate lots. Difficult stains were removed and any necessary mending done. Then all white cotton and linen articles were steeped overnight in cold water to which some borax or dissolved washing soda was added; handkerchiefs were steeped separately in cold salted water. Early the next morning the real work began. Water was heated in large coppers. The clothes were squeezed out of the steeping water, and they were rinsed. The

HOUSEHOLD BROOMS AND BRUSHES.

Aphis Brush 1/4	Brooms, Birch, for Garden use ... each 0/5
Billiard Board Brush 6/0	,, Carpet Whisk, American Flat ,, 1/5
,, Table ,, ... 7/2	Crumb Brushes 3/6 4/3
Black Lead Brush, for putting on black lead	Curtain Whisk, Flat 0/7½
0/4, or per doz. 3/8	Decanter Brushes 0/4 0/6 0/8 1/0
Bottle Brushes ... 0/1½ 0/2 0/3 0/4 0/6 0/8	

Bass Broom Heads ... 0/11 1/3 1/8 2/0
,, ,, per ½ doz. 5/3 7/3 9/9 11/9
,, ,, for stable use, each 2/9 3/3
,, ,, per ½-doz. 16/0 19/0
Handles for do. 0/2

Hair Broom Heads, 2/3 2/9 3/3 3/9 4/3 5/0
Per ½-doz. 0/1 each less.
Handles for do. 0/2

Turk's Head,
. · 3/5 4/8
Poles for do., 6 ft.,
8 ft., 10 ft., 0/1½
per foot. Poles,
10 ft., jointed, 2/2

Wall Broom, soft White
Hair, with 6 ft.
bamboo Handle 3/3 3/11
Do., with 12 ft. jointed
Handle 4/2 5/6

Whisk, with Velvet Protector Carpet
Broom · 2/9
Large size 3/9

Parquet Floor Broom, made of Cotton
Yarn, specially adapted for sweeping
polished floors, walls, etc. Price with
Handle, 3/0. To order.

Wall Head, Grey Bristle ... 4/10
Poles for do., 6 ft., 8 ft., 10 ft., 0/1½ foot.
,, 10 ft., jointed, 2/2

The Easy Grip Banister Brush,
Whisk, 2/2 ; with Plush Guard, 2/5

Banister Brush, Hair ... 2/0 2/4 2/10
,, Whisk ... 1/4 1/9 2/3

Marlboro' Whisk
Carpet Broom. 2/9
Large size. 3/9

Double Banister, Hair ... 3/5 4/3
,, Whisk and Hair 2/5 3/0

In the days before vacuum cleaners, a well equipped household had to rely on numerous specialised brushes. The Army and Navy Store D'Olier Street (1909) listed ninety different types of brush in its catalogue.

tub was filled with warm water and the body-linen and bed-linen was plunged in and washed methodically with soap, rubbing one surface on another, or perhaps using a washboard.

The clothes were then given a second wash in very hot water, more soap was applied if necessary; they were then rinsed. In order to remove every particle of soap and produce a good colour, they were put in a copper with some soda and boiled for about an hour and a half. They were then rinsed in hot water and an 'abundance' of cold water tinged with blue, after which, and weather permitting, they were put out on the clothes line to dry. The whole process was repeated for the table-linen, which, in addition, had to be starched, using boiling-water starch.

All clothes were made from natural fibres which required to be handled with great care. Woollens and flannels had to be washed very carefully in warm water to prevent shrinkage. Coloured garments, which could, and usually did, run, were also washed separately and kept well away from the other clothes. When it is remembered that all this activity took place in one moderately-sized kitchen and small scullery, that every drop of water was carried from one indoor, or perhaps one outdoor tap, first to be heated on the range and then emptied into the tub or sink, that the fire had to be kept red hot to boil water or clothes, that piles of clothes at varying stages of the process were strewn around, that two women, perhaps even one, toiled for hours, with bent back, in this hot, steam-laden atmosphere, it is not surprising that wash-day was considered detrimental to women's' health.

The expanding wardrobe

Just as eating habits at the time added greatly to the labour involved in preparing meals, the clothes worn in the 1850s exacerbated the ordeal of wash-day. As in home decoration, increasing prosperity also brought an increasing elaboration of dress. Skirts continued to expand; for the first half of the decade the desired effect was obtained by wearing a larger number of petticoats underneath. The weight of these finally became intolerable, and in 1856 they were replaced by a 'cage crinoline'. Flexible steel hoops hung by tapes from the waist, or were sewn into a petticoat. Women could now move their legs freely within their steel cage. However, there was danger in this and caricaturists delighted in showing what could happen to crinolined ladies in a strong wind. Legs were still supposed to be invisible, and in case the 'worst' happened, long linen pantaloons edged with lace and sometimes reaching the ankles, were worn. Not only were skirts enormous and often flounced, garments were trimmed with ribbon and lace which had to be removed and sewn on again every time the article was washed.

Men's clothes presented different problems for the laundress. Collars and cuffs and shirt fronts had to be starched stiffly and polished using a glossing iron, a tedious process, and one which continued well into the following century. Ironing was a difficult chore, and everything required ironing. All cotton and linen articles were sprinkled with water and rolled up tightly to give an even dampness, so that a smooth surface would be obtained when they were ironed. Flat irons, which were available in different sizes—larger heavier ones for flat work, small, four-inch, ones for tiny gathers, and fiddly parts—were usually used. They were heated on top of the range, and great care had to be taken to ensure that smuts did not ruin the clean linen. When the iron cooled, it was replaced by another hot iron. Box-irons were somewhat cumbersome to use, but were cleaner as the base of the iron was not in contact with the stove. They were hollow, and a slug of iron, heated until it was red hot in the fire, was slipped inside, and a door on the back closed. They also had the advantage of remaining hot longer. There were also irons for special purposes, such as the glossing iron already mentioned, and a goffering-iron for decorating frills on pillow-cases, night caps or other garments.

Daily life—the people at home

Victorian households tended to be large. Many sons remained at home until they set up their own establishments, daughters stayed at home until they married, and if they did not marry, remained on indefinitely; dependent relatives, mainly female, such as mothers, sisters, and sisters-in-law swelled the household number, and, of course, most suburban homes had at least one live-in servant. The saddest group of people in Victorian houses were the large number of unmarried women who were forced, by economic necessity, to live in other people's homes. These middle-class ladies were precluded by the mores of polite society from working outside the home. They greatly swelled the size of the Victorian household, particularly in the upper brackets. A small sample of houses from the 1901 Census reveals that twenty-four per cent of houses contained dependent women. Another sample, from the 1911 Census, showed that twenty-two per cent of lower-middle-class houses had dependent women (not including wives or daughters), thirty-eight per cent of middle-middle-class and fifty per cent of upper-middle-class houses.

Houses were rarely unoccupied during the day, because the housewife, servants, young children, and other female relations spent most of their waking hours in the home. In fact the home was intensely used—as living quarters, work-place, nursery, early school, and recreation centre. Servants at the beginning of the period might have had no free time, and never left the house except to go to church or perhaps to do some shopping. Their conditions improved towards the latter part of the century, but even then, they had at best one afternoon a week free, from after lunch, and every second Sunday afternoon. It is not surprising, therefore, that the dwellers in the new suburbs accorded so much importance to the home and lavished care and attention on its upkeep and adornment; apart from its symbolic importance, it was also the place where many of the family spent most of their lives. The physical separation of living from working, which the move to the suburbs entailed, led to a growing separation of the sexes to the point where, for the woman, the centre of existence became the home. To love and minister to her husband and children were the highest virtues and duties of a wife, and this required that she withdraw, to an extent, from the outside world, and restrict her work and social intercourse to activities based on the home.

Social life was carefully ordered and regulated by a recognised code of conduct. Rules governing 'calls', 'at homes', afternoon teas, dinners and parties were adhered to strictly, to avoid embarrassing mistakes. These sometimes expensive rituals were taken very seriously, and added not a little to the worries of a newly married couple with perhaps not quite enough money. A newly arrived family had to tread a wary path to enlarge its social circle from among the 'right people'. Even 'at homes' which were supposed to be casual, without invitation, were carefully planned to ensure that tea-tables were filled. To be presented to a stranger at a dinner-party was a guarantee of respectability which could then be developed in the ritual of calls: if acquaintance ripened, it would be recognised by an invitation to a dinner party, the apogée of the social scene.

Where sufficient trained staff was employed, the woman of the house could devote all her energies to managing the household, leisure activities, usually based on the home, and charitable work. The author's study of domestic service in Dublin showed that while ninety-eight per cent of the upper-middle class had servants, fully half employed only one or two; seventy-one per cent of the middle class had servants, nearly two-thirds having only one or two. In these cases the wife was involved in some of the household chores. Unless she had a professional cook, she probably played a part in planning menus and perhaps, preparing some of the more exotic dishes and the preserves. Meals were formal and elaborate, the family, apart from the young children, ate in the dining-room, the servants had their meals, either earlier or later, in the kitchen. Meals had to be served punctually, as punctuality was seen as part of a well-ordered life; a gong summoned all to the dining-room.

Daughters of marriageable age presented additional problems for their mother when she was compiling invitation lists to dinners and parties. Most upper- and middle-class girls remained at home when they completed their intermediate education, generally at fifteen to seventeen. After that their lives, like their mothers', were largely confined to the home, and opportunities for meeting the opposite sex were restricted to social occasions such as parties, dances and dinner parties. This was an enormous challenge to mothers, to contrive, without social blunder, the introduction of suitably eligible young men to their daughters. This was not only a strain on them, but also on their daughters.

Dances were often held for the purpose of bringing young people together. Large drawing-rooms with parquet flooring were ideal, rugs and furniture were removed or put to one side and professional musicians hired. If the drawing-room was carpeted, unbleached, figured damask linen was tacked on to the carpet to protect it. Most of the dances were waltzes and two-steps. Gallops and Lancers were kept to the end to use up the last ounce of energy. Supper was served at midnight in the dining-room and study; it consisted of cold dishes, chicken and ham and galantines, with fruit salad, cream and ice cream.

A cheerful gallop

Leisure hours

Most of the housewife's leisure hours were spent in the home, sewing or doing needlework, playing the piano or reading. At this time clothes were made by hand, and all female members of the family were expected to be proficient needlewomen. Their skill might be used to make shirts, underclothing, children's clothes, or indeed their own dresses and elaborate skirts; household linen and family clothes required mending. No drawing-room was complete without its sewing box or table. Of course, skill with the needle was a useful accomplishment for any young lady, who could while away her ample leisure doing embroidery, tatting, crochet, petit-point or knitting.

Books were usually borrowed rather than bought, from subscription libraries such as that run by Easons or Greenes, or for access to a wider stock from the London subscsription firm of

Mudies who would post a monthly box of books and journals. Newspapers were heavily taxed until the 1850s, but by 1855 stamp duty was effectively voluntary. By 1860 the *Freeman's Journal* was selling 1,230 copies a day through Easons, and *The Irish Times* nearly 1,900. In fact this was the trigger for a long growth in the importance and sale of newspapers in Ireland. By 1885 Easons were selling 7,400 copies of *The Irish Times* a day, and nearly 11,000 of the *Freeman's Journal.* Irish-published dailies were outselling English imports by 11 to 1.

As the century advanced, the infiltration of English culture, English values, habits, tastes, and goods increased, aided by better and faster communications. There was extensive circulation of British daily and weekly publications. Some children learned to read from English comics, such as *Comic Cuts* and *Chips;* others got their first ideas about school from the weekly *Magnet* and *Gem.* (C. S. Andrews, who fought on the anti-treaty side during the Civil War and later became the head of Bord na Móna, recalled that his life-time nick-name 'Todd' came from a character in one of these magazines.)

There was, of course, social life outside the home. There were occasional visits to the theatre, of which there were three in Dublin in the 1850s: the Royal, the Queen's and Dan Lowrey's. Dan Lowrey's Star Theatre, on Dame Street, which was succeeded by the Empire, had shows considered titillating and vulgar, not the type of entertainment the righteous middle class would consider suitable for wife or family. The Gaiety Theatre opened in 1872. It was built by the Gunn brothers, whose father died in the Portobello Bridge tragedy (see below, pp. 123–5). In the second half of the 1890s, it cost 1s 6d to see a musical comedy from the upper circle of the Gaiety—a day's wage for a well-paid working class woman. (The Abbey, which opened in 1904, was rather a special case.)

Dublin had two of that most British of institutions, the

music hall. The masses flocked to the Empire Palace and the Tivoli to hear vulgar jokes and ribald songs. The Gaiety, the premier place of entertainment, was famous for its annual pantomime, and relied on the visits of various English companies to put on minor drama, farces and musical comedy. From the mid 1870s, there were annual visits from the Carl Rosa Opera company and the D'Oyley Carte. For the more serious minded, there were productions of works by Shaw and Ibsen. The Theatre Royal, burned down in 1880, was reopened in 1897 as a 2,300 seater variety theatre offering musical comedy, and including shows such as wrestling, exhibitions by acrobats and performing dogs.

Dublin was a musical city, and had many musical societies, the Society of Antient Concerts, the Metropolitan Choral Society, the Dublin University Choral Society, the Philharmonic Society and the Madrigal Society, were just some which staged frequent concerts in the Antient Concert Rooms in Great Brunswick Street (Pearse Street). In 1861 Jenny Lind sang in *The Messiah* with the great baritone Belletti. There were three seasons of Italian opera in the Theatre Royal in 1859.

Highlights of Dublin social life, apart from the six-week Dublin Castle season, which started in February, were the Trinity College Races, held in June, and the Horse Show, towards the end of August. The undergraduates and their sisters, and the sisters of other undergraduates, the girls resplendent in filmy muslin outfits, enjoyed themselves to the music of a couple of military bands. The Park Races were collegiate and local, the Horse Show was not only national in its scope but international, and Kingstown harbour was crowded with the steam and sailing yachts of the very wealthy. Until 1881 the show was held in Kildare Street—in the lofty buildings used by the Duke of Leinster to stable his horses and house his carriages.

A simpler form of outdoor amusement was the Sunday

*The Horse Show was first held in Ballsbridge in 1881. It was a highlight of the
Dublin year for rich and poor, town and country, alike.*

promenade down Kingstown Pier from the Royal St George
Yacht Club to the lighthouse. The lady and gentleman, dressed
in their best outdoor attire, would walk sedately along the pier,
graciously acknowledging the nods and smiles of acquaintances.
Bands playing in public parks, such as Sorrento Park, Dalkey,
on Saturday nights, and the military bands, which were a great
feature of the summer months in Bray, provided much amusement for the young and not so young.

Towards the end of the century cricket, tennis and bicycling
were beginning to become popular. The Pembroke Cricket Club,
founded in 1868, was described two years later, as 'one of the
finest of our suburban cricket clubs' (*Pembroke Cricket Club
1868–1968*). Tennis and cycling had the advantage that they provided recreational outlets and social opportunities for women
as well as men. These more active past-times influenced the dress
of both sexes, but especially that of women.

Towards the end of the sixties, the crinoline disappeared altogether. It was replaced by the bustle; skirts became excessively long and trailing. Women continued to suffer from extremes of fashion, when, towards the end of the seventies and into the next decade, very long tight corsets were worn and waists were mercilessly tight-laced. A series of cartoon appeared in *Punch* showing women unable to sit down or climb stairs. By the nineties, skirts were bell-shaped and usually had a train even when worn on the street. In the 1890s the focus of fashion shifted to the top of the body and sleeves, narrow at the beginning of the decade, became very wide when the balloon sleeve was in vogue.

The new enthusiasm for outdoor sports made it necessary to wear more rational garments. There was a new vogue for the tailored suit, which consisted of jacket, skirt and 'shirtwaister'. Indeed when women went in for outdoor pursuits they insisted on wearing men's hats and men's stiff collars. It was impossible to ride a bicycle in a long skirt, so divided skirts and baggy knickerbockers were designed. These were ridiculed in the press and denounced from the pulpit, but young women continued to wear them. Male dress, which changed little from the seventies into the nineties, was also affected. The short jacket was becoming popular with the young, and the double-breasted 'reefer' jackets were also worn, especially for yachting. Special dress was devised for shooting and cricket. Bright coloured blazers were becoming fashionable for sport and visits to the seaside.

Special occasions which provided opportunities for family outings were exhibitions, inspired by the Crystal Palace Exhibition in London in 1851. The Dublin Exhibition of 1853 was held on Leinster Lawn and remained open for six months; a special Exhibition Hall was built in Earlsfort Terrace for the great Exhibition of 1865. These exhibitions were visited by royalty, Queen Victoria and Prince Albert, visiting the first, and the Prince and Princess of Wales attending in 1865. Right at the end of our period, in 1907, another great International Exhibition was held in Herbert Park. Among the exhibits were model houses of a markedly Edwardian character, and some of these were built, in Herbert Park and in Ranelagh. This Exhibition (which was attended by Edward VII, in a rage because of the theft of the so-called 'Irish crown jewels') therefore marks the end of the dominance of the traditional Victorian house we are celebrating.

Women, including grown-up unmarried daughters, especially in households where there were servants, must have found it difficult to pass the empty hours. Perhaps they played the piano (the upright piano was specially designed to fit neatly into smaller rooms), dabbled in water-colours and read the latest novels. They may have had some simple chores such as arranging the flowers; they, no doubt, had some social duties, making calls, and being 'at home'; however, the main socially-approved outlet for their excessive leisure, was charitable work. Doing good works also absorbed some of the free time of housewives, who in well-staffed, properly organised households may have found time hanging heavily on their hands.

The Rathmines Township Dorcas Aid Employment Society was typical of the type of work which absorbed the energies of leisured ladies. (Dorcas was a poor women mentioned in the Bible—*Acts of the Apostles* ix.36). It was founded in 1850 to provide employment for the poor by giving out needlework, which they would do in their own homes, 'thus enabling them, not only to add a little to their very scanty means of support , but also, infusing habits of industry among them'. There was need, it was said, 'for an increase of the benefits conferred on this deserving class of poor'. The ladies' committee met every Saturday from 11.30 am to 2 pm, in the Rathmines Township Female Schools, to dispose of clothing, take in orders and cut out garments, shirts, chemises, night-dresses, petticoats, drawers, pinafores and night caps. These articles were afterwards sold to the poor at reduced rates, and to others at cost price.

The master, the provider of the family house and all its comforts, was probably the one who spent least time under its roof. However, even when not at home, his existence was rarely forgotten; his wishes and convenience were of paramount importance when household arrangements were made. He was the centre around which the household revolved. Family photographs, which became popular towards the end of the 1860s, (in the 1870s family photographers had established their studios throughout the UK; William Lawrence opened his photographic studio in Sackville Street in 1865) made it possible to have the family group recorded for posterity. These showed fathers as confident, upstanding, middle-aged figures, surrounded by their loving and subservient wives and children.

Despite the *Skibbereen Eagle,* proverbially keeping its eye on the Tsar, world events were viewed with a certain detachment. Distances were great—even London was an uncomfortable, often rough, sea voyage and a tedious train journey across England away. Happenings nearer home were, of course, of greater interest. The Fenians, the disestablishment of the Church of Ireland, the Land War, Gladstone's Home Rule Bills, and the rise and fall of Parnell, especially his affair with Mrs O'Shea, provided lively discussion at dinner tables.

Some events made a lasting impression. Katherine Tynan recalled the bitter night in March 1867 when the Fenian rising was 'quenched in the snow', and how some of the vanquished, were creeping back from the Dublin mountains to their homes for weeks afterwards. She also remembered the outrages carried out in Dublin by the Invincibles. The Phoenix Park murders of Lord Frederick Cavendish and Under Secretary, T. H. Burke, on the 6th of May 1882, shocked Dublin. F. J. Little (writing in *Dublin Historical Record* vol. 6) remembers travelling on the early train to Malahide to meet his father for their usual Sunday walk. The people in the carriage 'looked anxious and uneasy', they 'conversed in subdued tones'. 'People gathered in groups at street corners.' It was only when he met his father that he learned what had happened. Katherine Tynan's father was driving home through the Park that lovely Sunday, when his pony and trap came on a police cordon 'drawn around the blood-stained spot'. The search had started for the weapons and murderers—the hue and cry lasted for many days.

Growing up in suburbia

Most children first saw the light of day in their own home (it was not until the 1920s that middle-class women began using maternity homes to any extent). The natural place to have a baby, or indeed, to be treated when ill, was in the comfort of one's own home. In September 1873, the Master of the Rotunda was called away from a dinner party to attend a lady in Sandymount, Annie Smithson's mother. He arrived in his brougham, still in evening dress, rolled up his sleeves, and left her mother with the memory of a diamond stud blazing in his shirt. It was usual for the first baby, or in a household where an experienced nurse was not employed for the other children, to have a trained nurse staying in the house for the first couple of weeks, until the mother felt able to cope.

The organisation and staffing of the home was, naturally, very much influenced by the presence or absence of children. If there were young children in the larger houses, the attic was usually their domain; here they spent their waking hours in the day nursery and slept in the night nursery next door. Their nurse, apart from some limited free time, spent day and night with her young charges. The young mother was advised that she should employ an experienced nurse, having got a good character from her last mistress, and if possible, seen the children she had reared. This seemed to be as much for the sake of the father, as for mother or child. 'The inexperienced and harassed young mother spends nearly all her time in the nursery, to the injury of her husband', and so she was warned not to 'neglect the big baby downstairs' (thus *Findlaters Ladies Housekeeping Book*). If, however, she could only afford 'a second-rate nurse', the mother had to supervise all the arrangements herself; in this case she was to take things coolly and not lose her head every time the baby cried. An infant's dress should be as light and as soft as possible. Flannel or flannelette were better than calico or muslin. The child must be kept warm at all times, (this was important advice when the trouble and expense of fires left many parts of the house very cold). Clothes should be left as loose as possible especially at night.

Ready for a walk

Families who could afford to usually employed someone to look after the children. Even lower-middle-class families were more likely to have a servant if they had young children, and that servant was usually a young girl to mind the children and help with the housework, while the mother did the cooking. Typically in such a household a servant was only employed while the children were young. In wealthier households, where a number of staff were employed, the children's nurse was generally a more mature experienced woman. Sometimes a nursemaid was also employed, to tend the fire, clean the nurseries, and generally help the nurse. In this type of home, children spent their earliest years in the company of their minders, confined to their own part of the house, and only saw their parents once or twice a day. In Eilis Dillon's grandmother's house, when the first baby arrived two nursery-rooms were set up on the top floor. Unfortunately, no extension was made when six other children appeared. A nurse and a nursemaid looked after the children, and the latter had to go up and down eighty-four stairs to the kitchen whenever necessary. Her mother recalled that if there was not enough food, nobody wanted to go down for

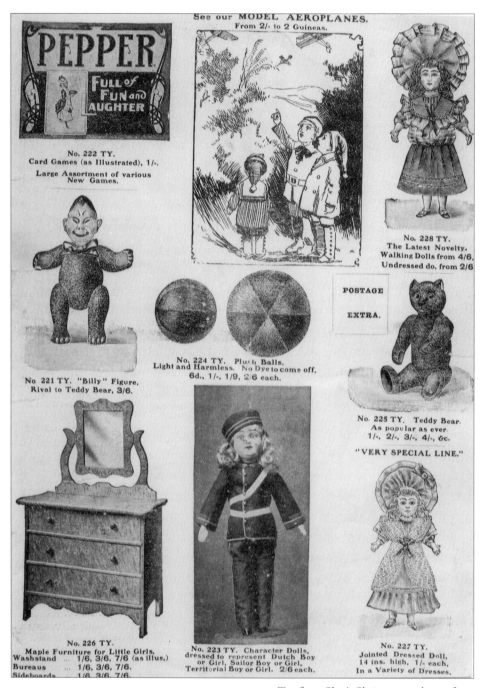

Toys from Clery's Christmas catalogue of 1909

more, so that the children were sometimes hungry. Clarke's 'Pyramid' nursery lamp, designed to keep food hot in a remote attic nursery, was widely advertised for just such a situation.

At noon every day, Eilis's grandmother went up 'all the way', as she put it, to the nursery to stay for a short while with the children. At six in the evening they were dressed up in their best clothes and brought down to the drawing-room for a short visit to their parents. As a general rule, the higher up the social scale, the less children saw of their parents.

As a result children often became more attached to a kind caring nurse, their constant companion, than to their distant parents, seen for short periods in the stilted and formal atmosphere of an intimidating drawing-room. Eilis's mother told how attached they became to Biddy who was with them for nine years; everything was clean and tidy, the daily routine ran smoothly, she played with them and took them for walks to the nearby park. Then her mother returned from Paris after an absence of several months, decided that Biddy was 'taking too much on herself', and sent her away. The children were devastated. To her mother, servants were 'different clay', as she said on numerous occasions; sacking Biddy was no more to her than 'if she had given away an inconvenient dog'.

If nurses were loving and efficient, children brought up in this way, were, no doubt, reasonably happy. If however, the opposite was the case, life must have been miserable indeed. Katherine Tynan mentions 'the terrors of childhood which are beyond telling'. Young children, led to bed by servant or parent, or later, when older, going on their own, through cold dark passages and stairways, lit only by the fitful flame of a single candle, must have imagined bogey men behind the folds of long heavy curtains and in every dark corner. Later lying wakeful in a pitch-black bedroom, separated from loved ones in the warm parlour below, by these dark impassable ways, every sound and

The governess and her chareges (1880)

creak became unimaginable horrors.

Life for young children was spent in the home, minded by mother or nurse. They played with their toys—dolls, dolls' houses, complete with furniture; rocking horses; wooden models of stage-coaches, carts, and trains; birds and animals on wheels, which the child could pull after him. Toy soldiers were very popular, originally the figures were flat, but at the end of the century, hollow, rounded figures were made. Soft toys were made by mothers skilful at sewing; golliwogs first appeared in the 1890s, and the teddy bear, called after Theodore Roosevelt, in 1903. Clockwork toys became available about 1897, and the clockwork train between 1904 and 1907. Wax was used to create babies or young children with chubby features. Previous to that, the only difference between baby dolls and adult dolls were the shorter limbs.

Education

Life was not all play. A state-supported system of primary education had been established in Ireland in 1831 (almost forty years before Britain). However, the majority of the upper and middle classes received their first education at home from resident governesses or visiting tutors. A school-room was set up, complete with desks and blackboard, probably in the converted day nursery on the top floor. Here the governess, and it generally was a governess, held sway. This was one of the few positions open to genteel ladies who had fallen on hard times, whose fathers, perhaps had died leaving them penniless. They may have answered an advertisement, such as one quoted in *The Lady of the House*, 'Good governess wanted. Ranelagh. Two hours daily (Saturday excepted). 15s monthly' (*The Irish Times*, 15 July 1908).

Lessons were held in the mornings, with the governess coping as well as she could with the needs of the different-aged children. In the afternoons, if she was a member of the house-

hold, she brought her young charges for a walk in the neighbourhood. Thus Miss Wallis would dress up the young Elizabeth Bowen in gaiters (pinching her calves with the buttonhook)
and her outdoor coat with a scarf before venturing out to the
exciting mysteries of Baggot Street. Otherwise, another member of the staff accompanied them. Middle-class children also
attended some of the many privately run schools. In 1855, Miss
Lydia Hopper ran a preparatory school for young gentlemen at
31 Castlewood Avenue. At 20 Leinster Road, Miss Nickson
had a ladies' seminary, while at Number 156, there was yet another preparatory school for young gentlemen, run by Mrs
Delamouse. Mrs Elizabeth Mahony ran a ladies' boarding and
day school at 80 and 81 Rathmines Road. The Rathmines Township Sunday and Daily Schools was at Number 122.

*Music was an important part
of a young girl's education in
the 1870s.*

Katherine Tynan, who left school at fourteen, said of the
young ladies' school to which she and her sisters were sent, that
it was 'one of those places of genteel inefficiency to which, in
Victorian days, they sent children to get them out of the way of
their elders.' Anyone could set up these schools, qualifications
were not necessary. At the age of fourteen, Annie M. P. Smithson
was not getting any education, so her mother decided to get a
German governess, take in little pupils and set up a school; Annie
could attend the lessons. It was not a success, only one pupil
enrolled. The education of girls was not taken too seriously in
those days. Eilis Dillon's grandmother was educated 'spasmodi-
cally' at home by her brothers' tutors, it was not considered
necessary to make special provision for her. When she was sixteen she was sent to a boarding school run by the Sacred Heart
nuns at Roehampton, south of London, for a year; this was
done, not for the sake of her education, but to remove her from
the unwanted attentions of a number of suitors. In between she
had a few terms at the Sacred Heart convent, Leeson Street, and
two terms at Mount Anville.

A limited education in the social skills, and to a lesser extent, the domestic skills, was deemed sufficient for the role of wife and mother, to which all girls were expected to aspire. So, in addition to literacy and numeracy, middle- and upper-class girls studied art, music, needlework, foreign languages and the social graces. Obviously, if the teachers were good, these subjects had an enriching effect, but vast areas of knowledge remained unexplored.

For boys, education normally involved being sent to school for several years. At the beginning of Victoria's reign, Catholic intermediate schools were few. The other religious communities were comparatively well served, mostly by schools long established under charities or by statute. (Many of the grander parents sent their boys to English public schools.) In the second half of the century this changed. Between 1850 and 1867 twenty-seven new intermediate schools, under the direct control of the Catholic Church, were founded; among them were Newbridge College, started in 1852, and Blackrock and Terenure Colleges, in 1860.

Older children returning from school were left to their own devices, to entertain themselves as best they could. Stephen Dedalus said his evenings were his own for reading. Reading seems to have been the main way of passing the time, especially on winter evenings. Some children had a large library at home into which they could delve. For others, in the days before public lending libraries were introduced (the first two municipal libraries were opened in Capel Street and Thomas Street in 1884), procuring books was a problem. Annie Smithson read novelettes belonging to the servant girl, and bought *Ally Sloper*, which she described as a vulgar English comic. Penny story papers were also available, such as *The London Reader, The London Journal,* or *The Family Herald.* Katherine Tynan's mother considered these even worse than the novels she read, so she had to read hidden behind the curtains, under the table, or in the loft over the stables.

In the most select neighbourhoods, children did not play on the street. Louie Bennett said of Temple Road: 'a sort of hush lay upon the road. Children did not romp there.' They played in their own garden with their brothers and sisters, ball games, such as croquet, or they skipped, played with hoops, or invented their own games. At times there might be more exciting things to do such as boating on the Dodder, or cockle-picking on Sandymount strand. On Sundays, children went to church, usually with their parents. Parents might also bring them for a walk, or for a ride in dog-cart or pony and trap to the countryside, or perhaps, the Dublin mountains.

Christmas was magical—coloured lanterns in the hall, living rooms festooned with boughs of red- berried holly, mirrors and pictures draped with ivy, perhaps a brightly decorated Christmas tree in the corner, and all seen by the light of softly-glowing oil lamps and blazing wood or coal fires. The excitement of opening presents was long remembered. Katherine Tynan's father bought the Christmas toys and decorations for the tree in the Cave of Aladdin, near Pim's drapery store in South Great George's Street. She recalled the toy of 'that' year was a parson with an ass's head; the head screwed off and the hollow body was full of sweets. 'That' year was probably 1869, as disestablishment of the Church of Ireland happened in July, when the Irish Church Act became law. She said it must have been 'very popular', as her father, who was no bigot, bought several of these semi-ecclesiastical figures. Less well-off parents bought 'little parcels from the Penny Bazaar: picture books, a tin trumpet, a little engine for Claude, a wax doll for Ella' (as Norah Hoult writes in *Coming from the Fair*).

Later in the day older children joined their parents for the traditional Christmas dinner of roast turkey with chestnut stuff-

Swimmers had been released from bathing machines, but not from cumbersome costumes (except, it seems, for the very young).

The ever-popular sailor suits first came into vogue when the Prince of Wales was fitted out in one as a boy.

ing, boiled ham and vegetables. Then, to the children's delight, the smiling cook arrived with the large round plum pudding studded with blanched almonds and sprigs of holly, and enveloped in a bluish flame. Another big treat was a visit to the pantomime. Katherine's father hired three cabs to bring his eleven children to the Theatre Royal.

Holidays were often spent beside the sea, in the vicinity of Dublin, at places like Seapoint, Bray or Howth. A house was rented for a couple of months. The family would usually travel by train; a special 'long car' met the train, this was described as being 'the length of three ordinary outside cars', and it had a deep well in the centre, where the children often sat with the luggage. The children swam, made sand castles, went for long walks and had picnics. Annie Smithson's grandfather rented a house, facing the sea, at Seapoint, for three months; she remembers wearing large straw hats known as Zulu hats.

The sheer elaboration and formality of Victorian dress did

not always sit naturally on the young, though clothes were simplified somewhat for children. Toddlers, both boys and girls, wore dresses, which were made very simply, with a plain bodice and a full pleated skirt. Warm dresses were made of wool; summer dresses, in bright coloured lighter materials, perhaps trimmed with velvet ribbon, and with short sleeves. It was a big day for the boys, when at the age of four, they were promoted out of skirts and put into knickerbockers. Broderie anglaise embroidery, which came into vogue in the late 1850s, became very popular for toddlers' dresses and for the front panels and edgings of baby gowns.

Young girls' dresses did not change much between the 1840s and the '60s, with variations in fabric and trimming rather than shape. Bodices were long; skirts were very short, often only to the knee, with the ends of broderie anglaise drawers showing beneath. Skirts became, like women's, very full, with a recommended width of 94 inches for an eight-year-old girl. The eldest girls' dresses were distinguished from their mothers' only by their slightly shorter length, and by the choice of less ornate material and trimmings. In the early 1870s plain muslin, worn with contrasting silk ribbons, became fashionable. In the following decades, developments in adult clothing—the introduction of knitted garments and the spread of tailoring for women—made girls' clothes more comfortable.

A little boy in the 1860s and early 1870s might be dressed in knickerbockers, shirt, waistcoat and collarless jacket, bow tie, long stockings or socks and boots. The suit might be made of velvet and trimmed with braid for special occasions. Knickerbockers were gathered at the knee. During the 1870s this fashion changed and boys' trousers were cut straight across, just below the knee. Boys might be dressed like their fathers, in long trousers, shirt, waistcoat and jacket. The sailor's suits, first worn by Edward VII when a young boy, started a fashion which was to last many years, well into the next century.

Out and about

Most of the suburbs, which developed from villages around Dublin, had clusters of small shops, which expanded in size and number with the influx of people from the city. Thus Baggot Street became the main shopping centre for the Pembroke township, though there was a village at Irishtown and there were a number of shops, provision dealers mainly, on roads, such as Haddington Road. In 1855 Baggot Street, Upper and Lower, had fifteen provision dealers, grocers or purveyors, a number of them selling wines and spirits; five victuallers; four bakers; two fishmongers; three confectioners; two poulterers, one also selling game; a dairy; three wine and spirit merchants; four chandlers and four apothecaries, two also described as accoucheurs.

Baggot Street was well able to supply the everyday needs of the residents in the surrounding roads. In addition there were a haberdasher and milliner; linen draper, haberdasher and stationer; ladies' outfitting warehouse; a shop selling baby linen and corsets; two ironmongers; china and glass warehouse; a tobacconist; general merchant and two post office receivers.

On the other side of the city, Fairview had two victuallers, four grocers, a boot maker, a tailor and an upholsterer. Rathmines was a busy shopping centre before the middle of the century. The opening of Alex Findlater and Co., general grocers, wine and spirit merchants, at 9 Rathmines Terrace in 1839, the second branch of twelve opened in our period (the first was in Kingstown in 1830), shows how quickly the suburb was developing and that its potential must have been evident. The advent of Edward Lee and Co. (Ltd), about 1890, brought a large drapery and furniture store to the area and meant that the residents could purchase all their normal requirements within the township.

The inside and outside of two of Findlater's famous chain of grocery shops, which grew as the suburbs grew. By 1907 there were 12 stores across the city.

Provision shops varied in size from the tiny local shop in the front room of a terraced house to large well-stocked stores such as Findlaters. The grocer's assistant had plenty to do, because every item on the customer's list had to be separately weighed and packaged. Although branded goods became increasingly common, items such as tea, sugar, spices, butter and flour were generally sold 'loose', small amounts wrapped in a dextrously twisted cone of brown paper. Teas were specially blended by each grocer to suit the water in the district. By modern standards, the range of merchandise may seem limited, but there was a wide choice of certain commodities. Findlaters sold nine different kinds of sugar: good loaf for preserving; finest broken lump, second quality of the same; lump (dust) castor sugar; icing; crystallised demerara; finest white crystal; crusted sugar and candy. There were sixteen different spices, a choice of almonds in seven different guises. *The Lady of the House* in 1891 carried five and a half pages of small print advertising for Findlaters' grocery department; four and a half pages were devoted to the wine department. Most people went to medium-sized, family-run shops, with mahogany counter, behind which were rows of drawers, filled with nutmeg, cloves, cinnamon, raisins, sultanas, currants and gelatine, with giant tea canisters overhead. Large bins for flour and sugar stood on the floor. Hams, sides of bacon and fly papers hung from the ceiling. Goods were weighed on a large scales with polished brass pillar using an assortment of brass weights. Behind the shop was a store in which firewood, paint, ironmongery, bacon and butter might be stored.

When Stephen Dedalus' grand-uncle brought him to the shop in Blackrock where the family dealt, to get the daily messages, he helped Stephen to whatever was exposed in open boxes and barrels outside the counter: 'he seized a handful of grapes and sawdust or three or four American apples'. The shopman 'smiled uneasily' and, when Stephen feigned reluctance to accept, said, 'take them Sir, they're good for your bowels'.

Elizabeth Bowen and her nurse did their shopping in Upper Baggot Street, which she called 'the Grafton Street of the trans-canal'. Everything was in its way 'classy': white coats of shop assistants were 'chalky clean, and sweet dry sawdust covered vict-uallers' floors'. Everyone had not only manners but time; 'we nearby residents made this our own village'. Those recalling the shops of the nineteenth and early twentieth centuries mention the smells, a powerful aid to memory. 'Every wine-merchant's exhaled a waft of mingled sawdust scent and strange mysterious breaths of vinous fumes'. Tea and coffee also 'paid aromatic trib-ute to the wayfarer', while confectioners 'crowned all this odor-ous feast', spices also played their part. Bowen also mentions the cake shop in Baggot Street, though, as the cakes were made in their own kitchen, they were not regular customers, 'how dear to me was its spiced baking smell!'

The manuals advised housewives not to waste too much of their time shopping. A respectable servant could be trusted to do the marketing. (Indeed this bit of patronage was a favourite cook's perk. There was much indignation in kitchens through-out the land when the Christmas boxes given by tradesmen to cooks were prohibited by the Prevention of Corruption Act 1907.) Groceries should be ordered in fairly large quantities for delivery on a certain day and a standing order left at the grocer's. Butter was better bought at one of the dairies, if bought from the provision dealer it could have the taste of some of the other articles in the shop. Perishable goods had to be purchased more frequently. Greengrocers, butchers, poulterers and fishmongers called at houses in the morning and took orders, in this way housewives could order what they wanted for the following day. Some poulterers even brought around the fowl to the door so that a selection could be made.

While there were some haberdashers and millinery shops in the larger suburbs, most people went, as Bowen said, into the city: 'For hats and coats and things that were more momentous we made the journey to the real Grafton Street.' At this time men's clothes were made by the tailor, and the majority of middle-class women went to the dressmaker and milliner. *Thoms* listed 174 milliners and dressmakers in Dublin city and suburbs in 1860. Women made the journey into the city to choose fabrics and trimmings for their new outfits. The advent of the sewing machine from the late 1850s onwards revolutionised the making of clothes, which up to that time were all sewn by hand. So, as the century progressed, ready-made clothes became more common.

Department stores/monster stores

The industrial revolution had led, not only to the mass production of necessities formerly made in the home, or by local craftsmen, but to the production of a range of new articles which created new wants. For the first time shoppers were exposed to the display of a wide variety of merchandise at relatively low prices. It is not a coincidence that the development of the de-

McSwiney and Delany's New Mart, or 'monster store', opened just in time for the visitors to Dargan's Exhibition of 1853.

partment store or the monster house, as it was called, dates from this time. Four, smaller in scale, already existed in Dublin when the New Mart, the store which became known as Clery's, opened in 1853. It was intended from the beginning to eclipse anything that already existed in Europe, where department stores were also a new phenomenon. It was a distinguished, five-storey building, with an arcaded, high-ceilinged, ground floor, fronted by a balcony. It was grander than anything in London, and ante-dated the Bon Marché in Paris, erected in the 1860s; the store often cited as the origin of the modern department store. The monster store had the advantage of selling a variety of goods under one roof and of being able to display these goods to advantage. As a measure of their impact, there was a ten per cent drop in the number of independent milliners and dressmakers in Dublin between 1860 and 1870. They introduced the idea of shopping as a past-time, and, no doubt, the concept of impulse buying.

The monster houses stressed the idea of shopping as a leisure pursuit; like their counterparts in the United States, they presented the home-maker with a cornucopia of goods, like a permanent International Exhibition. This was well worth a journey into town in omnibus or carriage. The growth in population in Dublin City between 1850 and 1900 was very small, so these stores depended on the rapid growth of the suburbs, especially those on the south side of the city. The customers of the new monster stores, drawn, it was estimated, from the upper eight or ten per cent of the population, sat on bentwood chairs at mahogany or glass-fronted counters while deferential shop assistants displayed the range of goods from which the customer might, or might not, decide to purchase.

Getting around

Those who went shopping on foot in nineteenth-century sub-urbia, had to contend with the dust from the roads and streets in the dry summer weather, and the mud and the puddles when it rained. Roads were surfaced with road metal, which was crushed stone, and frequently developed pot-holes, which were filled in roughly with loose metal, left to be ground down by the hooves of horses and the iron tyres of drays and carts, so that 'after rain no man could cross a street dry shod'. It was much more difficult for the women with their long skirts, they had to seek out the crossings, which were paved pathways; in 1847 it was decided that there should be six crossings on Rathmines Road, three of which were opposite the Catholic Church, Barrack Road Gate, and Findlaters. Even the footpaths were often in a bad state; in Rathmines from Findlaters' shop to the corner of Church Avenue, they were partly gravelled and 'imperfectly flagged'. It was decided that the part opposite the shops, about seventy yards, should be laid with granite flags one yard wide.

The main shopping streets in the bigger townships were noisy and lively during the day, with horse-drawn omnibuses plying to and from the city, delivery cars and milk carts, with large churns and brass taps protruding through the tailboards. At dusk, as the lamplighter went on his rounds, things became much quieter. People had to step with caution, as the light shed by the gas lamps did little to dissipate the darkness. It was only in 1884 when the incandescent gas mantle was invented, that gas light-ing improved, giving a more intense light and using much less gas. Street hawkers enlivened the residential roads as they plied their trade, calling, 'freestone, freestone' (used for scrubbing white deal kitchen tables); 'chairs to mend', 'umbrellas to mend'.

One of the reasons for the growth of the suburbs from the 1840s onwards was the development of public transport. The

Hallway in Avoca Terrace (Micheál O Nuallain)

Large and richly guilded mirrors were much favoured in Victorian homes, and complemented the fine mantlepieces. White mantelpieces were chosen for drawing-rooms while black or grey were preferred for dining-rooms. (Peter Pearson)

provision of stabling for horse and carriage, with, perhaps, accommodation for a coachman overhead, therefore, became much less important, and was confined to the really large houses. Annie Smithson's grandfather, who lived beyond Rathfarnham, where there were no trams, drove to his chandlery business in Capel Street every day in his own carriage. The Murphys, who lived near Louie Bennett on Temple Road, and were in business, had a brougham (four-wheeled closed carriage, having a raised open driver's seat in front) and pair, driven by a coachman in uniform and sporting a cockade on one side of his hat. They were considered very wealthy.

The omnibus drawn by two horses was used for public transport. From 1840 there was an omnibus service on four routes, Rathfarnham, Clonskeagh, Sandymount and Clontarf. The vehicles carried twelve passengers inside and ten on the roof. They had a narrow door at the back, small windows and straw on the floor, and were stuffy and uncomfortable. They were also not cheap—an 'inside' to Rathfarnham cost six pence, at a time when a labourer's wage was two shillings a day. Outside cars also plied for hire, carrying three people on either side at four pence each. By 1850 an omnibus service between Rathmines and the city centre had been established and ran every half-hour, and the fare was 3d. Five years later, the service had expanded, and the bus ran every ten minutes, with the same fare. For the prosperous middle-class business man, the cost of his daily journey to work, and his wife's occasional shopping trip to the city, was much lower than the expense of keeping horse and carriage and employing a groom or coachman. By 1860, Clontarf had an omnibus plying to and from Dublin every half-hour.

As usual, the safety of the travelling public only received attention when a serious accident occurred. A typical example was the appalling catastrophe which took place on Portobello Bridge on Saturday, 6 April 1861. Although newspaper accounts varied in a number of details the main facts were established. The 'Favourite No. 7 Omnibus' left Roundstown (Terenure) at 9 pm for the GPO; the driver and conductor were on the sixth run of their fourteen and a half hour working day. They picked up eight passengers on the Rathgar and Rathmines Roads. The bus stopped at Portobello Bridge, on the incline at the Rathmines side, to drop a man and his son. Then the conductor gave the signal 'all right' to the driver to proceed. One of the horses refused to answer the bit and commenced backing, helped by the incline and dragging the other horse with him. The driver, as was usual in such cases, tried to get the horses across the road, and succeeded in getting their heads turned towards the Charlemont Canal, but the horses continued to back. The conductor had jumped from the bus when it started to move backwards, closing the door behind him. In answer to the driver's cry to 'hold the horses', two men grabbed the horses' heads, but to no avail. The omnibus, driver still in his seat, horses and all went into the lock chamber. The lock depth was twenty-five feet and it contained ten feet of water at the time. The driver was hauled to safety.

The few who witnessed the accident 'if not rendered powerless by the sight, ran for assistance'. When the news spread, people gathered, the crowd looking down, according to a contemporary source, 'into the deep chasm, the darkness of which was dimly revealed by a solitary lamp, half-lighted by contract, on the bridge above. No voice issued from the vault of death below.' A loud splash, followed by a faint snort from one of the horses, was the 'only sound to emanate from the gloomy gulf'. Candles were obtained to enable them to see 'the half-floating tomb'. Then, instead of opening the sluices of the lower level and letting the water out, the lock-keeper opened the sluices of the upper gates, in the hope that by letting water in the bus might float. This did not happen, and the difficulties increased.

Ultimately, the water was allowed to subside and the omnibus became visible, too late to save the six people within. Two men, a police constable and a private from the 4th Light Dragons, got on to the roof, and with butchers' hatchets smashed the roof. They removed the bodies, which were declared to be 'perfectly dead' when brought to the Meath Hospital at 10 pm that evening. From an early hour on Sunday until late that night 'successive crowds of people of all classes visited the scene'.

The inquest was held at the Meath Hospital, and lasted for three days, 8–10 April. The coroner addressing the jury said that, as far as he could see, there was no blame whatever attached to the Messrs. Wilson, who ran the omnibus service, their driver or conductor. He said the bridge had 'long been a nuisance and a disgrace to the neighbourhood'. The jury returned a verdict of accidental drowning—'we do not attach any blame to any persons concerned, believing that all exercised themselves to the best of their judgement on this sad occasion'. They suggested that the attention of the Rathmines Commissioners should be directed to the unsafe state of Portobello Bridge and 'the great want of light thereon', and said that the public should be protected from a reoccurrence of accidents 'on this much-used thoroughfare'. The repercussions of this disaster were felt for a very long time in the area. Passengers on horse-drawn vehicles, had to alight at Portobello Bridge and walk across the bridge before continuing their journey to or from the city.

The advent of the horse tram in 1872 caused a stir in the city because it entailed laying tracks on the streets. F. J. Little remembered seeing, from his nursery window, the tracks of the first tram being laid down in St Stephen's Green. The work continued at night by the 'smoky light' of crude paraffin flares. The first horse tram travelled from College Green to Garville Avenue on the first of February, taking twenty minutes to complete the journey. 'The insides of the cars', said the *Dublin Daily Express*, 'are richly cushioned in velvet, and fitted all round with sliding plate glass windows.' The harness of the horses was trimmed with red facings to which little bells were attached. A high tariff of three pence, for even a short journey, was charged, putting them beyond the means of the working man or the servant girl. *The Irish Times* was critical of the venture. It questioned whether the one pair of horses provided for each tram would be sufficient. Actually tip-horses had to be used at eight or nine points around the city, including Portobello Bridge, Baggot Street Bridge and Charlemont Bridge, to help the trams up gradients that were too steep for the ordinary team of two. By 1881 the Dublin United Tramways Company operated 186 horse trams and had over a thousand horses. Passengers could get on and off the tram wherever they pleased, and staff were told to: 'Keep a sharp lookout for passengers, and by signalling, induce persons to travel who would otherwise walk'.

Enter the machine, slowly

With the coming of the electric trams at the end of the century, the last horse tram was taken off the road on 13 January 1901. The change-over from horse traction to electricity was slow. It began in the suburbs. The electric tramway from Haddington Road to Dalkey was opened in May 1896. A tram ran every ten minutes, from 8 am to 11 pm. The *Freeman' Journal* complained that this was too early for theatregoers—they omitted to say that many working people would like an earlier tram. These services were catering mainly for the middle classes in the new suburbs. The fare to Merrion was a penny, to Kingstown, three-pence, and to Dalkey four pence—a scale of fares that remained the same on this line until the First World War. The electrification of the whole system followed, working as before from the suburbs inwards. The first Dollymount car arrived at Nelson's Pillar on 20 March 1898, to be followed in July by the first car from Dalkey.

Various rudimentary types of bicycle existed from the beginning of the century, the velocipide, with wooden spokes and wooden tyres, truly christened the 'bone-shaker', gave way to the 'penny farthing'. However, it was only in the seventies— when geared wheels of equal size were connected by a chain, and the modern bicycle was born—that it became popular. It provided a cheap method of travelling to work for the suburban dweller; it also made weekend excursions to the country and the seaside possible. The rough state of the roads made bicycling an activity for the younger and fitter members of the population. The motor car was introduced into Ireland in the second half of the nineties. At a cost of about £268, it was only for the better off. It was less expensive to run than a brougham and two horses, which it replaced, and had many other advantages.

Bicycles provided a new independence and freedom, especially for young women.

Technology advances

Electrical telecommunication became a reality during Queen Victoria's reign. The first commercial telegraph in Ireland, in 1851, ran along the route of the Midland and Great Western Railway, between Galway and Dublin; it was run by a private company, as were all the early operations. In 1852, the first cross-channel telegraph was completed—from Holyhead to Dublin. When the omnibus accident occurred at Portobello Bridge in 1861, the telegraph service was used to inform the husband of a mother and daughter who perished, who was in the west of Ireland at the time, of the tragedy. Private operation of the telegraph did not result in a full service, and in 1870, the Post Office took over the telegraph network, with a brief to provide a service to the whole country. This it did, and the telegraph rapidly became a reliable, accessible and affordable method of communication, which by the turn of the century, reached the most far-flung parts of the country.

The first telephone exchange was opened in Dame Street, in 1880, and initially had only five lines. Growth was slow, by 1888 there were only 500 lines and three sub-exchanges in the Dublin area. The telephone made very little impact on the lives of suburban residents; the telegraph service was of much greater importance to the late Victorians. Even by the late 1920s advertisements for the telephone were still pointing out that one could call the fire brigade, the police, order the groceries, book a table in a restaurant, arrange a game of golf or hire a domestic servant, if one had this device.

Mechanisation of the household came very slowly. There were still nearly three times as many servants per head of the population in Britain than in the United States, where labour-saving devices were much more common. In Britain it was not until after the First World War, when servants turned in their thousands to other occupations, that housewives had to look seriously at easier ways to run their homes.

A long period elapsed between the introduction of gas for lighting and its use for other purposes, such as cooking and heating. A few cooking appliances were shown at the Great Exhibition in 1851, but none of them was taken seriously, and gas refrigerators were only developed in 1922. It was only in 1907–8 that people in the more prosperous areas of Dublin city and suburbs, such as Merrion Square, Northumberland Road and Highfield Road, started to use gas for cooking, heating and water heating. It was really only with the coming of electricity to the home, and the application of the small electric motor to vacuum cleaners, washing-machines, food-mixers, sewing-machines, floor-polishers and dish-washers, that household labour was lightened significantly. This also happened slowly. In November 1911 there was an electrical exhibition in the Mansion House, Dublin, at which electric cookers, hot plates, and fires were exhibited; it is clear from the catalogue that these appliances were new to most people at the time. It was only in the mid twenties that the public was beginning to realise the advantages of using electricity for cooking, heating, washing, ironing and vacuum cleaning.

To ease that most difficult of household chores, many efforts were made to produce hand-operated washing-machines. Several different types were invented, none was really successful. It was said of one of them in 1922 that 'the labour needed to work the hand-operated machine is so little short of hand washing that they have never come into general use.' So at the end of our period, when the International Exhibition in Herbert Park took place in 1907, the enormous changes in communications, sanitation, transport, new inventions and social relations that were to characterise the twentieth century were just beginning to show themselves. But there was some way to go before a recognisably 'modern' world was to appear. Father still dominated, mother stayed at home; servants were still regarded as essential to the running of the middle and upper-middle-class house. Streets remained dirty, skirts remained long.

Enjoying the long Edwardian afternoon

Looking after a Victorian house

Peter Pearson

A Tudor-style house in Ranelagh, typical of the late nineteenth century.

Terraced brick house, Rathgar, c.1830. The first developments of the early 1800s in places like Rathgar were closely modelled on the Georgian tradition. Houses were still built of brick and the house was fitted with Georgian sash windows. The pillars of the earlier period about the doorcase gave way to wooden panelled pilasters with carved brackets.

By now it will be very clear that the Victorian period was one in which the new middle classes came into their own. Their houses, with their fine facades, flights of granite steps up to the front door, elaborate ironwork, rich interior plasterwork and elaborate gardens, were carefully and proudly embellished to reinforce the status and position of their owners. The challenge for us in the late twentieth century, is to be able to live in such old houses, complete with anachronistic features such as electricity, central heating, running hot and cold water etc., while restoring and conserving the authentic feel of the original building.

Victorians relished a wide variety of choice as regards architectural style; the grander houses were built in the Classical style, in the Georgian style, the Tudor style, the Gothic style and possibly even a French or Continental manner. There are many examples of all these styles throughout County Dublin. For instance, in the 1830s a successful manufacturing chemist named Charles Leslie built for himself a villa in a rather severe Classical style on land overlooking the sea at Dalkey. He called the house Carraig na Gréine and it was entirely built of cut granite. At about the same time the wealthy land-owning family of Shaw built for themselves Kimmage Manor and chose an elaborate Tudor-style residence. The Tudor style was particularly popular for large detached residences, perhaps because it reflected an age of wealth and elegance in England, which many owners wished to emulate. Old Conna, a house near Shankill, was one of the most extravagant examples of a cut stone Tudor mansion, elaborately decorated with oak panelling, tiles, stained glass and Tu-

Many Victorian architects were very fond of richly decorated pilasters such as this one which is part of a bay window.

dor-style plasterwork.

Another example is St Luke's Hospital, Highfield Road, Rathgar, which began as an elegant Victorian house with much Classical detail and a stunning interior. St Luke's, originally called 'Oakland', was built on the site of an eighteenth-century house of which there is now no trace. It was later occupied by Charles Hely, the owner of the successful and well known Dublin stationary and printing firm located for many years in Dame Street. It was a very large house, with extensive wings, servants' quarters, nine family bedrooms, three large receptions rooms, a billiard room, eight servants' bedrooms, kitchens, pantries and flats for four gardeners. The most astonishing feature of St Luke's is its painted, stuccoed and gilded ceilings, which were installed by Hely in 1895. The principal drawing room, with its bow windows, is richly ornamented and painted with pictures representing the seasons. The plasterwork is in the French style and is gilded, even the backs of the drawing room doors are decorated.

Clontarf Castle was completely rebuilt in the early nineteenth century in the Tudor style while Roebuck Castle, which is now part of University College Dublin Law School and stands on its Belfield campus, is another example of the lavish stone-built architecture of the nineteenth century. The facades feature highly carved decorative Gothic detail with the initials of its owner worked into the stonework around the front door. The architects Deane and Woodward specialised in building houses in the Gothic style and one of the finest examples is Glandore in Monkstown, built in 1858 in the Venetian Gothic style. The house has a multitude of tall chimneys, pointed Gothic windows and Gothic-style balconies.

The Victorians in general loved decoration and colour and they particularly liked richly plastered interiors, coloured fanlights and the decorative ironwork that was used for balconies and lamp standards. We shall examine these elements in more depth shortly. The richer citizens could spend extravagantly on the houses, and their houses themselves reflect this by having more turrets, grander porticoes, bigger conservatories and finer entrance gates.

By far the majority of the 35,000 or so Victorian houses in Dublin, however, are much less grand than these. They were built in groups of two or more, often by a small speculative builder, and with very little attention from a trained architect. Walking along such streets as Ashfield Road or Beechwood Avenue in Ranelagh, the eye learns to pick out these groups. Even though at a casual glance within these groups the houses look uniform, there are myriad small details of difference in the presentation of windows, in the framing of doors and steps, in the decorations of walls. It is easy to spot the houses that were built together (in these cases in the 1890s). Many of the more ordinary Victorian houses in Dublin have excellent plasterwork, fine joinery and sometimes richly coloured glass windows. There were very few badly built Victorian houses, and the fact that so many have lasted for so long is a testimony to their builders.

One particular model or type of house became very popular in the middle of the century. This was the villa, with its hint of the gentleman's country residence and often designed to look larger and grander than it really was. The original urban villas consist of one storey only over a basement, often with a valley roof. The roof is sometimes hidden from passers-by by a parapet. The principal reception rooms were located on the first floor and were reached by means of a flight of granite steps, while the ground floor was used for the kitchen and the extra bedrooms that might be needed. The villa usually stands alone but was sometimes terraced or semi-detached. Features of the villa, notably the granite steps leading to the reception, were repeated in multi-storied houses, such as those in the terrace of

This Victorian House, near Dublin Airport, is typical of the larger type of detached residence, with its solid proportions, painted stucco facade, bay windows and large porch. The first floor windows are ornamented by ornate pediments and there is a central canopy which covers a balcony.

Leeson Park, or North Circular Road, houses erected for successful professionals such as solicitors, retired army folk or the first editor of the *Irish Independent*. There are many outstanding examples of villas in areas such as Monkstown, Blackrock and Sandymount. Most of them adhered to the Classical style and had attractive columns or pillars around the door but some chose the more delicate Gothic form making use of decorative gables with barge boards and tall Gothic style chimneys. Later in the century builders abandoned the villa style, and opted for a simple ground-floor front door (putting the kitchen at the back of the house). There was, however, no reversion to the older, space-saving, style of stepping straight on to the street from the front door—a gentleman needed a front garden, however small.

The many terraced houses of Dun Laoghaire, or Kingstown as it then was, were built in a Classical idiom. The seafront

terraces of Dun Laoghaire and Monkstown, which were built
between 1830 and 1850, tended to be uniform in design and
interestingly were intended to be painted in a uniform colour as
well. Some of the leases stated that the houses were to be painted
every two years in Portland stone colour only. The style of these
tall terraced houses was restrained, sometimes having a Geor-
gian-style pillared doorcase with a fanlight or a large pair of
brackets on either side of the door. The redbrick houses of
Rathgar, Rathmines, or the Clonliffe Road in Drumcondra often followed the Georgian tradition by having an arched door-
way with a fanlight above.

All of the many Victorian terraces which were built throughout the suburbs relied on an element of uniformity to create a
successful impact. The unified terraces of Iona Road in Glasnevin
are a good example of this. An important ingredient in this
were the gardens in front of the houses with their cast-iron railings and stone plinths. (In some areas, such as Phibsboro, where
cattle were regularly driven through the streets to market or to
slaughter, the railings were a practical defensive barrier.) From
the grandest terraces such as those of Northumberland Road in
Ballsbridge down to the more modest rows of houses in
Drumcondra and Harold's Cross most have the standard Victorian railings set on a cut granite base.

The terraced houses of the seafront at Sandymount and
Clontarf also made much use of features such as bay windows
and decorative ironwork. Many houses had handsome balconies and these were usually based on Classical designs with panels featuring palmette or honeysuckle motifs. Sometimes Gothic
designs were also used.

In the later nineteenth century it became popular to use different colours in the facade of a brick house and a variety of
different shapes of brick were used. Sometimes Gothic arches
were made of mixed red and yellow brick used to great effect.

Restoring your old house—basic principles and guidelines

The principles of conservation, whether for the Custom House, a grand villa, a simple cottage or terraced house, are the same.

The first principle must be to carry out the least amount of alterations to the original fabric of the building, and to leave the building with a sense of its historic past by conserving as much as possible of all the original detail and design. This applies to the maintenance of the visual setting of the building with its garden as much as to the fabric itself. The entire frontage, including the adjoining houses with their railings, steps, trees and hedges are all part of the streetscape.

Another principle of all conservation work is that where essential elements are missing the features should be restored by replacing them with good replicas. If there is a damaged or rotten portion the best procedure is to replace those elements by copying a sample or keeping an existing moulding and giving it to the craftsman or builder who should be given careful instructions that a correct copy should be made.

Authenticity is an important goal. All too often incorrect or approximate copies are made of old details which can spoil the overall effect and the authenticity of the building. Equally, if brick or stone has been damaged or worn away and it is decided that it must be replaced the type and colour of the original should be matched as closely as possible. Several architectural salvage yards now stock a wide variety of old brick, but it is also possible to buy new bricks which can make a good match. Where a house is part of a terrace it is obviously very desirable to match any slating work or roof details with those of the neighbouring buildings.

The most outstanding message of conservation work is to repair rather than replace, so as to retain the character of the building. All too often interesting features such as old floor-boards or the original lime plaster of the walls are simply dumped in a skip without a second thought. This means that the feeling of age has been taken away from the building which is often a pity. The fact that a house looks and feels old is half the charm of living in such surroundings. Often a window frame or a plaster cornice may look totally beyond repair but usually, following a careful examination these details can actually be retained and repaired and there is often no need for total replacement at all. The result is a more authentic historic building which preserves its feeling of age and of history and respects the original craftsmanship.

Another important idea informing modern conservation work is that any new work carried out in the building should be reversible. In other, words, if it is necessary (which is unlikely) to partition a room with a beautiful ceiling, the partition should be inserted in such a way as not to damage any of the original fabric, so that it could be taken down at a later date.

Find out about your house before you start

Let us assume that you are seeking to restore your Victorian house as accurately as possible, and that you have enough time and commitment to do so. Obviously if your main concern is to prevent the roof from leaking on a new-born baby, and you are on a tight budget, some of the finer principles of conservation may have to be left aside until time and money allow. However, in an ideal world, the first step should be to find out as much as possible about your house. Fashions in house design and decoration, as we have seen, did change quite markedly over the Victorian period. A house built in the 1840s is likely to be quite different in feel and presentation to one built thirty years later. For example, the earlier house will generally tend to have ornamentation of a simpler kind, whereas by the 1880s the taste was for heavy oak staircases and bold wallpaper design. In other words, in pursuit of authenticity, it is worth finding out what are the typical details of, for example, a hall door in a terrace of 1860s period houses, or what are the correct plasterwork details for a building of that date.

It is desirable also to understand the history of the building and to assess its present condition before beginning work. Not only does this greatly add to the interest of the work, but also expensive mistakes can be avoided. There are architects and other specialists who have particular skills in working on old buildings and old houses and if in doubt their advice should be sought.

Before you start, take a series of photographs of the house and garden, inside and out. Any large-scale works or alterations should be carefully recorded and documented by photographing the work both before and after the event. Even on a modest project it may be useful afterwards to have such a record—not to mention the satisfaction such 'before' and 'after' photographs can provide.

Roofs

The first job to tackle is the roof. It may seem very obvious to say so, but many owners of old buildings will carry out a great deal of expensive work and even decorate rooms while ignoring the state of the roof above. The helpless horror of a leak suddenly sprung through a split in the leadwork of the valley, letting water cascade down the carefully decorated walls and soaking into rugs, is not a happy experience.

If the roof is faulty in any way, if the valleys are leaking, if there are defective slates, sooner or later damage will be caused. As well as normal wear-and-tear problems can arise, for instance, from poor DIY work of the previous owners, or even from heavy-footed cable-TV operators. Look out for damaged or slipped slates, cracked renders, damaged leadwork or chimney stacks in poor condition. The most common causes of prob-

Modern substitute slates are best avoided on important historic buildings, especially where the roof can be seen, or is part of a terrace.

A badly repaired and maintained valley roof, with a mix of asbestos slates and thin, cracked and broken modern slates. Rainwater has collected on the poorly maintained valley, where no doubt the lead is torn leading to water leaking into the roof and attic space.

The importance of regular roof maintenance cannot be over emphasised!

A good example of a dormer window in a Dun Laoghaire terrace of late nineteenth-century red brick houses.

lems with roof structures are woodworm and dry rot and in severe cases they can lead to the complete destruction of the timber structure; however, it is usually possible to treat affected timbers without having to completely replace the structure.

Another common problem with roofs and chimneys is where the lead flashing around these elements has become damaged or porous and sometimes these can be replaced without a whole-sale re-roofing job being involved. Other problems are caused by blocked chimneys, blocked rainwater pipes and leaking plumbing. Crows have a habit of building nests in chimneys and the buildup of their debris can cause water to leak into rooms in the house.

Step one therefore is to check the roof.

Regular maintenance of roofs is equally important. Few owners of houses enjoy cleaning out gutters and valleys and sweeping out leaves that might block the downpipes. However, if such simple tasks are not carried out on a regular basis serious damp problems can soon arise.

Most Victorian houses have slated roofs which vary in their complexity. Some elaborate Tudor-style houses have many pointed roofs, gables and small porches which will require an even higher level of careful supervision. But the average terraced house usually has a fairly simple double pitched roof.

If a roof has to be replaced, and this may not always be necessary, old slates or good quality new slates should be used. It is possible to source second-hand slates, but only good quality ones must be used. Thin, flaking or cracked slates are no use. Also, a variety of new slates are now available, at moderate cost, and these may be used as a second choice to using re-cycled slates. The use of synthetic slates, with their too-perfect uniformity of shape and shade, detracts from the overall appearance of the house, especially where the roof is visible.

A few Victorian houses have tiled roofs which can look extremely attractive and generally seem to last very well. Terracotta tiles including fancy ridge tiles are often an attractive feature and these of course should be retained. Some highly elaborate roof structures were slated with different coloured slates in bands and it would be worth preserving or reproducing this feature.

Chimney pots and chimney stacks are also a significant feature of such houses. Throughout the Victorian era *all* heat for cooking, washing or warmth, came from lit fires. Throughout the year, at least one coal fire was constantly kept burning in every house—in the kitchen—and frequently also in other rooms. The chimneys therefore had a vital role in drawing all the smoke thus created out of the house. This in turn created the famous urban fogs of the period, such as the London 'pea-souper'. Even if the chimneys are no longer in use, the visual impact of the chimneys is a critical part of the overall design of the house and they should be preserved.

There is a great variety of design in chimney pots and many salvaged pots can be sourced to replace your damaged originals. Some new pots are also made and exact replicas are available from specialist suppliers. Other features of roofs such as dormer windows should also be retained and add greatly add to the attractiveness of a building.

Water, water

In our climate, attack from water, whether in the form of rain or rising through the foundations, is one of the great threats to a house's integrity. Cracked or damaged rain water goods such as drain pipes are probably the most common external source of dampness in old houses. In the nineteenth century most rain-water goods, gutters and hoppers were made of cast iron. In general cast iron gutters and rain pipes survive very well, but if they are cracked or damaged they should if possible be replaced with replicas. Several companies specialise in replica cast iron products of this kind. Plastic pipes and even aluminium replicas are best avoided.

A cast-iron water hopper. The lead roof flashing has become detached.

To control other water attack, a few simple rules should be observed by the owners of Victorian houses. All leaks or signs of dampness should be carefully explored and the source of the problem identified. Any damage to slates and roofs, gutter etc. should also be attended to without delay. Valleys and gutters should be kept clear of leaves and other debris. Again the general principle of minimum intervention should be adhered to and if replacements are necessary they should be carried out using proper replicas.

More insidious is rising damp, one of the most common problems in all old buildings. Walls built in the nineteenth century did not generally have any form of damp proof course, although sometimes slates were laid at the bottom of the building in the stonework. Rising dampness can cause many problems including powdering of paint and plaster surfaces and can lead to timber decay in floors. This can result in wet rot, which simply destroys the strength of the timber. Affected areas should be removed and the source of the damp eliminated.

Here again there are many methods of dealing with the problem. Specialists argue about the efficacy of one method over another. There are various waterproof substances which can be used but they may in fact cause more problems than they solve. Electrical systems can also help to prevent some rising damp and some people have found them very successful while others wouldn't touch them. Each case must be tackled after carefully examining the nature of the building and its location and in many instances there will be a simple reason for the dampness; for example, it may be caused by the build up of earth on the exterior wall.

There is a common misconception that the stripping off of old plaster and exposure of stonework underneath will cure such dampness, but in most cases the plaster will be necessary to weatherproof a random rubble wall. Walls which were built of rubble stone were never generally intended to be left exposed except perhaps in the case of an old mill building or industrial building. In general, the use of strong Portland cements are not advisable on the walls of old buildings as they tend to trap moisture in the wall and prevent the wall from 'breathing' and prevent damp from evaporating.

As we have seen, it was not until quite late in the century that Victorian houses were equipped with anything more elaborate in the way of plumbing than a cold tap in the kitchen. For any house built before the 1880s, therefore, internal WCs and baths with running water are likely to be late innovations, which may or may not have been well installed. Leaking plumbing can often be a simple problem but one which can cause horrific damage if it is not attended to.

The bathroom came into its own as a proper room in the last decades of the nineteenth century. This coincided with the more plentiful supply of piped water and the availability of a wide range of enamelled bathroom products. Deep cast iron baths were often set into a timber surround, while others wree left free-standing in the middle of the room. Some baths had attractive feet in the form of lion's paws, while others incorporated large, somewhat intimidating shower units! Some of the older taps and plugs on these baths are worth re-conditioning.

Bathrooms and toilets may well be happy hunting grounds for unusual wash basins, baths, toilets and Victorian tiles and there is now a very wide range of replicas available, some of them being remade by the firm of Minton or Doulton who produced them first over a hundred years ago. Toilet bowls are also worthy of consideration as there are some highly decorated and interesting examples to be found in the most unlikely places. Sometimes the interior of the toilet bowl was decorated with flowers or other pretty motifs! Some of the leading bathroom and tile stores now stock good replica fittings of this kind.

Dry rot

Perhaps the quietest, most unobtrusive and yet destructive attack on your house comes in the form of dry rot. It can completely destroy timber and even mortar in the structure of a building. Dry rot is a form of fungus and will only thrive in the right environment, this environment needs dampness, warmth and darkness for the fungus to flourish.

In the past it was common practice to drench buildings in various chemicals, and this, apart from the health risks involved, often caused damage to plasterwork and other surfaces. There has been much debate about the different method of treating dry rot, but all are agreed that the most important first action is to eliminate all sources of damp and to air the building or area affected. In some large buildings it may be worth installing an electronic monitoring system which will alert the owner to the presence of damp and so prevent a possible outbreak of dry rot. Areas affected by the fungus should be removed, and rotten timber burnt. Limited use of chemicals may help to kill the fungus spores.

Outside walls, brickwork, cement finishes and mortars

Though a great number of Victorian houses were built of brick, the use of cement renders was also very popular, particularly in coastal areas. In places such as Dun Laoghaire, Blackrock and Dalkey there are many examples of Victorian houses which were built of rubble stone, after which they were plastered or rendered and finally painted. This material was sometimes known as Roman cement, a sort of brownish, red coloured, very hard plaster and was very commonly used for decorative features on Victorian houses. Roman cement is not generally available today, but some specialist firms in England do stock it.

The Victorians loved ornament and so this cement which could be cast into various decorative features (and architraves) found itself used for window mouldings, doorcases, projections over doors, canopies and large cornices at the top of buildings. Often the corners of buildings were marked out with coigns and the windows themselves were articulated with strong mouldings made of Roman cement. The result could be buildings of great decorative quality though sometimes the decorative elements could deteriorate if not maintained. These elaborate features can be repaired or copied faithfully and replaced.

It was also popular to strike out the lower floors of the building in bands or lines in order to simulate stonework, and equally many rendered surfaces were struck out in blocks again to simulate stonework. Glass-reinforced concrete has been used quite successfully to reproduce some of these mouldings where they are lost. However, care must be taken to prime such mouldings carefully before painting as there may be various chemical residues in the paint which will lead the paint to peel off.

A fine example of plasterwork, in this case a decorative scroll at tha base of a window in a terrace house in central Dublin.

Many more modest Victorian houses such as cottages and farm buildings were rendered with a simple lime-based mortar known as rough cast. A rough cast render was generally made from a coarse sand or a mixture of pebbles which was added to lime putty and then literally flung on to the surface of the wall. This attractive finish, which was usually whitewashed from time to time, can give great character to an old cottage or farm building and should be carefully preserved or replaced.

A third category of finish for walls of buildings is stone or brick which is pointed generally by a lime-based mortar. However, during the last thirty years there has been an unfortunate tendency to use very strong cement mixtures for pointing both brick and stone. This practice can lead to much damage, especially to brick where the top surface can eventually flake away due to the retention of salts and water in the wall itself. A correct mixture for pointing brick or stone must be found, and should be based on a weak mix using lime mortar. The general

An example of the worst type of cement pointing on old brickwork. Not only does it look ugly but it also endangers the brick.

An example of a more appropriate form of pointing using a soft lime mortar

rule with pointing is that it should be discrete and not stick out proud over stone or brickwork.

The excise duty on bricks was abolished in 1850. In the Victorian period bricks began to be made by machine and became very even and regular often with a glazed or shiny appearance. There were many brickworks in Ireland during the nineteenth century and some of the best known in Dublin were Dolphin's Barn and Mount Argus and in Wicklow, Bog Hall in Bray. In Belfast the Annadale Brickworks specialised in making highly decorative bricks and mouldings to be used on Victorian houses and other buildings; some of these bricks featured rope mouldings, special key stones for over doors and decorative panels for the middle of the wall; other bricks for cornices and mouldings around windows were also made.

Sometimes brickwork can become disintegrated and decayed and it can either be replaced by accurate replicas or sometimes carefully repaired using a repair mortar which can be coloured to match. As already mentioned, some salvage yards stock bricks which may match those in your house. There are several methods for cleaning brick and stone and these include careful water washing, some chemical treatments and some mild abrasive cleaning methods. The cleaning of brickwork should be approached with great care, because some harsh methods of cleaning, such as grit blasting can actually cause irreversible damage to the surface. Chemical cleaning should also be approached with caution and may sometimes lead to damage if it is not carried out under expert supervision.

Victorian Dublin possesses a limited number of impressive stone built houses, but these naturally enough require great care when tackling cleaning or pointing of stonework. The two most common stones used in the Dublin area are limestone and granite. Nearly all Victorian buildings have some granite used perhaps as window sills or as a flight of steps up to the front door.

Again the cleaning of such stone work should be approached with great caution and may not always be necessary at all.

If there is damage to stonework it is important to seek the expert advice of a stone expert conservation architect or stone mason who will be familiar with the materials and the types of problems. For instance, some of the older eighteenth-century granite is prone to damage and disintegration. Also various types of sandstone are very soft and can literally erode away to nothing in the present climate of air pollution. As in the case of brick, it is also possible to splice in pieces of matching stone where the original is totally disintegrated. It is also possible to use repair mortars and these can often be quite economical and very successful.

Many of the grander houses in areas such as Clontarf, Blackrock and Monkstown made use of more unusual stones such as red sandstone and Portland stone. These stones generally survive quite well but can sometimes be affected by air pollution.

A typical mid-Victorian terraced house, with its generous flight of granite steps leading up to the hall door, rendered facade and Victorian sash windows.

Windows

After heat, a household needs light. Although electricity was available at the very end of our period, for virtually every household artificial light meant first candles then gas or oil lamps which were both smelly and expensive. Natural light was therefore at a premium. Of course, just as today, builders struggled to retain decorum and privacy while maximising light.

This struggle makes the windows one of the most significant features of any house. If any kind of authenticity is to be preserved, the importance of retaining the original windows, or at least of having correct copies made, cannot be overstated. Unfortunately, all too often original features, and in particular windows, are ripped out of Victorian houses and replaced by unsympathetic materials such as uPVC or aluminium.

During the eighteenth century it was only possible to make

glass in quite small sheets and this led to the manufacture of windows which had small panes giving us the characteristic 'Georgian' window which normally consists of two sliding sashes made up of six or nine panes each. In the nineteenth century, as a product of the Industrial Revolution, 'plate' glass was invented, so in about 1840 large clear sheets of glass became available and many of the Georgian houses of Merrion Square and elsewhere replaced their older windows with these new large-paned windows instead. Excise duty on glass was abolished in 1845 and window tax in 1851. It was the fashion for most houses built from 1830 onwards to have plate glass windows, especially in the main facade, whereas sometimes the older type of windows were still installed in the back of the house, presumably because these were cheaper to make. In the old Georgian windows the hand blown or wavy glass was generally used. In some cases attractive old panes of glass still survive in eighteenth-century windows. But even in Victorian windows, certainly up until about 1860, the sheets of glass were also slightly uneven and wavy which creates a delightful play of light on the window. The glass then is also an important part of the original fabric of the building and should not be discarded unless it is badly damaged and beyond repair.

The windows of Dublin's Victorian houses are usually of the sliding sash type. This means that they slide up and down on weights, which are concealed in a box either side of the window behind the shutters. The sliding sash window is a feature of houses in Britain and Ireland, and is part of the overall design and appearance of the house. In this we differ from our neighbours in France and in Southern Europe where windows are generally 'casement' types, which means the windows open in and out rather like a door. The typical window consists of two sashes made of timber with a large sheet of glass in each, sometimes sub-divided into two separate panes, creating a four-paned window altogether. Sash windows are meant to glide up and down easily so it is important to make sure that the pulleys and weights are all working properly.

Often people will discard windows thinking that they are rotten, when close examination will often show that it is only the surface or the paint that is decayed and the timber of the window itself is in good condition underneath; even if the bottom rail of the window is rotted or damaged it is possible to repair it by splicing in a new piece of timber.

If the owner decides to keep the original windows of the house, which should be the case, what can be done to keep out draughts or stop the windows rattling? There are many different systems for restoring windows one of which is the well known 'Ventrolla' system which involves the careful insertion of a draught-proof strip and the repair of the windows themselves. This means that the windows are sound-proofed and draught-proof while preserving the original fabric of the building.

For those who might think that to purchase new timber windows will be very costly, it might come as a surprise that the construction, particularly of a Victorian window, is a fairly simple operation. There are many good joinery shops who can now make accurate Victorian windows at a reasonable price. Also, many of the plastic-coated windows may only have a life span of twenty or so years, perhaps a little longer, whereas a good timber window has been shown to last up to 200 years if it is kept painted. Plastic windows cannot be painted, and the double glazing of such windows makes escape during fire something of a problem.

An important part of the Victorian window are the pair of shutters which are generally to be found inside; sometimes these shutters have not been used for years, but it is generally quite an easy operation to get them working again. Shutters provide a useful measure of insulation and also give a level of security

A Georgian sash window; note the six panes of glass in each sash and the fine panelled shutters.

Typical Victorian windows were composed of two sashes, each glazed with a single pane of glass.

when they are closed. The painting of windows is a subject of some debate, especially in Victorian houses. The general favourite is to paint windows white or cream, but sometimes stronger and darker colours can look very well on buildings which are of a lighter colour.

The bay window was another feature which could almost be described as a Victorian invention and many Victorian terraced houses and detached houses used the projecting bay window as a means of getting side-long views of the sea or simply to admit more light into the rooms. Such bay windows were often constructed entirely of timber.

Ironwork

Though not so crucial to the life of the household as the chimneys and windows, decorative ironwork strikes an important note in the way a Victorian house presents itself. There will probably be railings along the front garden, a more or less elaborate gate, perhaps more railings leading to the hall door, and maybe a boot scraper to remove as much as possible of the mud of the streets. The design of boot scrapers can be quite varied including honeysuckle patterns, leaves and even animals. Another item of ironwork which was sometimes decorated was the lid of the coal hole. This circular disc of iron gave access to the coal cellar and was often decorated with oak leaves or some similar motif. Dublin is fortunate in having a wealth of fine ironwork unlike London where so much ironwork was scrapped and melted down for armaments.

There are essentially two types of ironwork, wrought iron and cast iron. Wrought iron, as the name implies, was made by a blacksmith working on the anvil. The iron would be heated up and beaten into the required shape and the pieces might then be riveted together and made to form a gate or lamp standard. Wrought iron is difficult to snap or break but is prone to corrosion and rusting. Cast iron, which became popular in the nineteenth century, involved the pouring of molten iron into a mould, thus enabling multiple copies of a particular object to be produced quite quickly. There was a great variety in types of

Elaborate cast iron lamp brackets such as this one were available from the catalogues of iron foundries.

Decorative cast-iron railings

cast iron and several iron foundries made a good business from supplying types of gates, railing heads and decorative gas lamp standards. Designs in railing type included such motifs as the fleur de lys, the spear, the urn and Gothic motifs. A wide variety of decorative products were available for architectural purposes, including street furniture. Much cast iron has lasted extremely well but it is prone to being broken or snapped. To repair such a piece an entire replica piece would have to be made.

The furniture of the hall door might also be made of cast iron; knockers vary in design considerably, but the most common are the Dublin female head, the wreath knocker, or the hand holding a ball. Larger houses might well have elaborate gas lamp standards sometimes supported by figures such as dolphins. Cast iron was also used in the construction of conservatories and glasshouses and there are some outstanding examples in the Dublin region. For example, a unique circular conservatory may still be seen at the Loreto Convent in Bray, but the largest and most elaborate of such structures are the various glass houses at the Botanic Gardens in Glasnevin.

The usual problems with ironwork are those of missing elements, broken pieces, overpainting and rusting. Ironwork whould be thoroughly stripped and cleaned from time to time and carefully primed and re-painted. Wire brushing and careful abrasive blast cleaning can be used to clean cast and wrought iron. As a general rule it is better to apply a number of thin coats of paint rather than a few thick coats. There are now a number of specialist craftsmen who restore ironwork and it is possible to order replicas of some Victorian examples.

Interiors

Perhaps as a reaction to the relative coolness of the Georgian interiors, and perhaps partly as a response to the new range and variety of goods available, the style and decoration of Victorian houses became increasingly heavy and rooms became very

Classic wallpapers from the 1860s (Barry Mason)

Staircase and window, typical of the 1850s, with wide mahogony handrail, cast-iron stair balusters, and a standard Victorian window, in Deansgrange House, now demolished (Peter Pearson)

crowded with furniture, hangings, pictures and other objects. The general ambience was one of clutter and rich confusion. The formal, ordered layout of eighteenth-century rooms became a thing of the past. As the nineteenth century wore on the taste for more sombre colours grew and with it a liking for embossed wallpapers, linen crusta and stencil work.

The Industrial Revolution made a huge range of goods available to the new middle classes. It was possible to buy a much wider variety of furniture, wallpaper, mirrors and pianos, than had been available before, as well as mass-produced light fittings, decorative tiles and fabrics. For many these objects would have been first seen at the great industrial exhibitions, or at the new 'monster stores'. Catalogues, such as that produced by the Junior Army and Navy Store in d'Olier Street, were produced from the 1880s onwards which showed the great array of goods which were available.

These mass-produced goods were not always well made or well designed. William Morris was the prime mover in a campaign to combat what he saw as a flood of poor design and badly made furniture and other objects. Morris encouraged artists and designers to go back to nature for their inspiration and only to accept the best of craftsmanship. Some examples of Morris style tiles and wallpapers may be seen in Victorian houses

The Junior Army and Navy Stores in D'Olier Street sold a wide variety of fire furniture, including fenders, fire irons, pokers, fire dogs and fire screens. These trivets were for keeping plates and teapots warm.

in County Dublin, and where they exist they should be carefully preserved.

It is, of course, rare to find a Victorian interior which has survived completely intact. However, various elements may be seen in old houses and these may include the original pelmets, light switches, fitted bookcases and old wallpaper and fireplaces. Victorian wallpapers have not survived particularly well, partly because they were printed with thick paints and inks onto thin papers and damp conditions often led to the flaking of such wallpapers if not their complete disintegration on the wall of the house.

There are probably few undiscovered houses with rooms decorated with Victorian wallpaper, but should such an example be found it would be well worth restoring. The restoration of wallpaper, as with any antique paper, is a specialist job and advice should be sought. There have been rare instances in some houses when wallpaper was removed to reveal murals beneath, as a small number of houses were decorated with mural paintings. Such paintings were generally of a decorative nature and often depicted scenes of the Italian or Swiss alps.

Fireplaces

The centre-piece of most Victorian rooms is the fireplace. During the nineteenth century the taste developed for a heavy style of fireplace, with elaborate grates and surrounds which themselves became increasingly elaborate. Following scientific principles, the open hob grate disappeared in favour of a closed, sometimes arched, grate which was situated quite near the floor. Cast iron units eventually began to become more and more decorative with the inclusion of panels of tiles at either side of the grate. Early grates sometimes incorporated a small trivet, which was a small stand on which a teapot could be stood to keep the tea hot.

The actual fireplace surround in Victorian times became extremely elaborate and sometimes rather fussy and decoration varied from Tudor motifs to the more usual rope mouldings and floral designs. Some grates contained a hood which could be pushed up and down to control the flow of smoke. The cast iron or brass fender was another important piece of fireplace furniture. These were also available in a wide variety of designs. Towards the end of the century, the mantlepiece became elaborate, at the very least being adorned with a fringed cloth, a clock and statuettes and other ornaments; the most elaborate versions combined a mirror and numerous alcoves and decorations in wood. Mantlepieces continued to be made from marble, at least in the finest rooms, but towards the end of the century, cast iron and oak fire surrounds became ever more popular.

An example of heavily over-painted plasterwork from the underside of a staircase. The crisp detail will only be visible again if the plaster is carefully cleaned.

The decorative tile is one of the most outstanding achievements of the Victorian period. Tiles combined attractive designs with great colours, and could be used for floors in entrance halls or conservatories or for lining the walls of bathrooms and decorating the sides of fireplaces. Many tiles derived their designs from plants and flowers, but the variety of Victorian tiles is very extensive and there were tens of thousands of different designs available. Floor tiles, which tended to be thicker than other types, were generally of a geometric design and earth colours were favoured. William Morris also popularised many new tile designs concentrating on images drawn from nature, such as the orange tree.

Plasterwork

The eighteenth-century tradition of decorative plasterwork did not completely die out in the nineteenth century. In fact, many Victorian houses have extremely fine examples of plasterwork in principal rooms and hallways. Most Victorian houses have elaborate cornices and fancy centre pieces in the middle of the ceiling; these features are sometimes damaged and small pieces may be missing. It is a relatively simple job to replicate missing elements and put them back as part of the overall restoration process.

Most Victorian plasterwork is made of plaster of Paris which can be quickly reproduced in many interesting forms. One of the most common forms of ceiling rose is a centre piece composed of up to eight elaborate leaves. The leaves were commonly modelled on the Acanthus plant although others were also used and sometimes a stylised form of foliage would be interspersed between the leaves creating a highly decorative effect. Other patterns involving scrolls and vines might be entwined around the ceiling rose to make a greater impact. Other popular motifs in plasterwork were vine leaves and sometimes Gothic elements.

In very elaborate houses, plaster was often used as a decorative device over the doors, these being known as over-doors. Another popular feature was a continuous frieze of vine leaves and grapes or perhaps a string of ivy leaves with little clusters of ivy berries. It can be easily seen that there was huge variety within the repertoire of plaster workers and Dublin is particularly rich in Victorian plasterwork detail.

The cornice of the room, which is the meeting place between the ceiling and the wall, was the place for an elaborate treatment, usually consisting of egg and dart mouldings, dentils and perhaps a row of small rosettes. These small rosettes were normally cast individually with a little nail or piece of wood sticking out the back; they were then individually stuck into the cornice. If any of these are missing it is a fairly straightforward job to make new casts and simply replace them.

The actual cornice was generally run *in situ*, this meant that the plaster was built up in layers on wooden laths with a heavy layer of lime mortar first and a finishing coat of plaster of Paris. The modern method of using a fibrous plaster mould can be successful, but is best avoided when dealing with repairs.

Apart from the problem of missing features in decorative plasterwork it is also very common to see ceilings heavily over-painted which can lead to the total obliteration of all the detail. Cleaning the plasterwork to reveal the detail can be quite easily achieved provided hard gloss paints or others have not been used. There are quite a number of specialists in the field of cleaning and restoring plasterwork and if in doubt the correct procedure would be to call in an expert for advice. Sometimes the simple application of water can be used to clean plaster, but usually stronger substances such as Nitromors or specialist chemicals may be needed; once again caution must be used otherwise permanent damage can occur. The rule for conserving plasterwork must be the same: only replace when necessary and only do so by copying existing models.

Ceiling roses became more and more elaborate during the nineteenth century. They were designed to concentrate the centre of the room and ornament the point from which the lamp hung.

Appendix 1: Exploring the history of your own house and street

Start with the first Ordnance Survey map of Dublin (see pp 5–6), which was published in 1838. This will tell you whether your house actually is Victorian. Then look up the address in *Thom's Directory*. Thom's took over the publication of the Post Office Directory in 1844, and is an invaluable source of information. A full series is available in the Gilbert Library in Pearse Street, Dublin 2, telephone (01) 677 7662. This will enable you to check the names of occupiers over a number of years. In some instances it will also give his or her occupation. Check on the names and occupations given for adjoining houses; note how frequently they change, the large number of households that were headed by women, and the large number of vacant houses. As the location of the Corporation's library service Dublin collection the Gilbert Library has an extensive collection of books and other sources on Victorian Dublin.

The 1901 and 1911 Census Enumeration Forms (the forms filled in by the householder) are available in the National Archive, Bishop Street, Dublin 8, telephone (01) 407 2300. This will give you the name, age, religion, occupation and place of birth of the inhabitants, and the names of resident servants. Again, it would be interesting to check the details for adjoining houses. The National Archive also holds extensive maps and written records relating to the Pembroke Estate.

Ask your solicitor for copies of surviving old legal documents relating to your house. The building lease will provide the names of the ground landlord and whoever erected the house, plus any requirements concerning design, materials and adjoining properties. It is also worth examining old wills, indentures or mortgages relating to the property. If these are not available, you could search for documents in the Registry of Deeds, Blackhall Place, Dublin 7. Such records provide some interesting details concerning the lives and financial arrangements made by Victorian families.

For more general information about housing and building, look up the *Irish Builder*, (originally the *Dublin Builder*). There is a set in the Irish Architectural Archive in Merrion Square, telephone (01) 676 3430, which also has an archive with files and photographs of interesting houses and terraces in Dublin. The Dublin Civic Trust, 4 Castle Street, Dublin 2, telephone (01) 475 6911, is also recording Victorian buildings, and provides information to the public on conservation.

The following is one brief example of what can be learned from the wills, deeds and indentures relating to one house.

In 1867 John McCurdy, an architect, undertook to erect three houses on the north side of Belgrave Square in Monkstown; the sites were leased from Robert Gray of Temple Hill, Blackrock for 900 years subject to an annual rent of £6 17s 6d per site.

When his only daughter Mary Agatha McCurdy married the Dublin merchant Adam Findlater in 1881, he settled an annuity of £100 on her for life, which was to be paid from the rental of these three houses. According to the marriage settlement there was a clear profit of over £200 per annum on the houses at this time. In the event of his daughter's death, the annuity was to be used to support and to educate her children until they reached the age of twenty-one.

This settlement could be discharged at any time if her father paid £2,000 to the trustees of the marriage settlement. John McCurdy died in 1885. In his will he left the life interest in these houses to his widow Lucy, subject to the £100 annuity to his daughter.

His widow also inherited a life interest in three houses in Ailesbury Road and another house in Monkstown, the income from various investments in railway stocks and debentures, the proceeds of an insurance policy and absolute ownership of all furniture, plate, linen, pictures, clocks, books, horses, vehicles, harness, outdoor implements and greenhouse plants; he bequeathed his racing cups to his daughter. If his widow remarried, her daughter would receive half of the income from the houses and other investments. Otherwise his daughter would inherit a life interest when the widow died; following the death of Mary Findlater the life interest would pass to her children.

At no stage did any member of the McCurdy family live in any of these houses. Indeed it would appear that John McCurdy owned only one of the three houses in Monkstown, Blackrock and Dalkey that were given as his address during the years 1867–85; at the time of his death he was living in a rented house. In 1920, in order to sell the houses in Belgrave Square, his widow paid the sum of £2,000 to the trustees of her daughter's marriage settlement. By then Mary Agatha Findlater, a widow, was living in Golder's Green in London.

Appendix 2: Select list of specialists in conserving and repairing Victorian houses

The following list of reputable firms and individuals with experience of dealing with historic buildings was compiled from the lists produced by an Taisce, the Irish Georgian Society, the Dublin Civic Trust and the contributors' personal knowledge. The list is by no means complete— there are other reputable firms and craftspeople working in this field but this selection is a starting point for those embarking on restoring a Victorian house.

Architects
Contact the Heritage Council, Rothe House, Kilkenny tel (056) 70777 or the Royal Institute of the Architects of Ireland, 8 Merrion Square, Dublin 2, tel (01) 676 1703 for lists of architects specialising in the care of Victorian buildings.

Brass fittings
Repairs and new fittings
Healys, 51–54 Pearse Street, Dublin 2, tel (01) 677 2238

Conservation builders
The following are familiar with traditional building techniques.
Bow Street Construction, Quadmount Court, Chapelizod, Dublin 20, tel (01) 623 6640
Thomas Brennan, (Lectros) 105–7 Cork Street Dublin 8, tel (01) 473 4645
Gibson Builders, 6 Castleside Drive, Rathfarnham, Dublin 14, tel (01) 490 5433
Cleary Doyle, Larkins Cross, Wexford, Co. Wexford, tel (053) 20377
Lissadell Construction, 111 Ludford Road, Dundrum, Dublin 14, tel (01) 298 3610

Fanlights
Repairs
Alan Tomlin, Irish Stain Glass, The Studio, Treetops, Greenlands, Sandyford Dublin 16 tel (01) 295 6167

Ironwork
For repairs and replacements
Bushy Park Ironworks Ltd, 23 Greenhills Business Park, Dublin 24, tel (01) 462 2788
H & M Ironworks, Unit 2, Greenhill Industrial Estate, Walkinstown, Dublin 12, tel (01) 450 7072
Tony Heade, 31 Ennafort Park, Raheny, Dublin 5, tel (01) 831 3160
Harry Page, 67 Leeson Close, Dublin 2, tel (01) 676 6657
Cast iron gutters and drain pipes
J. J. Longbottom, Bridge Foundry, Huddersfield, Yorkshire, England, tel (0044) 01484 68214

Locks
Fogartys, 5 Crane Lane, Dublin 2, tel (01) 677 1961
'Interlock', 54 Temple Road, Blackrock, Co. Dublin, tel (01) 283 3544
The Lock Hospital, 49 Suir Road, Dublin 8, tel (01) 453 4544

Paint and interior finshes
Clements and Moore, Chelmsford Lane, Ranelagh, Dublin 6, tel (01) 491 0637

Mary McGrath, Rosetown Road, Newbridge, Co. Kildare, tel (045) 432 007
Plasterwork
James Byrne, 3 Clonnermore Green, Jobstown, Tallaght, Dublin 24, tel (01) 452 7981
Sean Henderson, 44 Gilford Road, Sandymount, Dublin 4, tel (01) 260 4292
Leddy Ltd, Highfield House, Highfield Park, Dundrum, Dublin 14, tel (01) 298 9375
Anne McGill, 1 Clontraf Road, Dublin 3, tel (01) 853 0439
Seamus Ó hEocha, Corbally, Barna, Co. Galway, tel (091) 590 256
Old Mould Co., 8 York Road, Dun Laoghaire, Co. Dublin, tel (01) 284 2777
Andrew Smith, Ballinakill, Kinnegad, Co. Westmeath, tel (0405) 39040
Paul Traynor, 47 Blackheath Park, Clontarf, Dublin 3. 833 6319
Roofs, slates
Crickley Roofing Ltd, 664 Ballycullen Road, Dublin 16, tel (01) 493 5816
N. Kelly & Sons, 87 Collins Avenue East, Killester, Dublin 5, tel (01) 831 6472
J. C. Walsh & Sons, 49 Arbour Hill, Dublin 7, tel (01) 679 3572
Stonecutters and suppliers
Kevin Corrigan, Stonescapes, 9 Parklands Rise, Maynooth, Co. Kildare, tel (01) 629 0812
Jason Ellis, 80 Aughrim Street, Dublin 7, tel (01) 838 6338
Feely Stone, Elphin, Boyle, Co. Roscommon, tel (079) 62066
Brian McAfee, 10 Cherryfield Road, Walkinstown, Dublin 12, tel (01) 430 2732
James Murphy & Sons, Murphystown Road, Sandyford, Dublin 18, tel (01) 295 6006
Patrick Roe, 181 Goldenback Cottages, Kiltiernan, Co. Dublin, tel (01) 295 9150
Stone Developments, Ballybow, Enniskerry, Co. Wicklow, tel (01) 286 2981
Stone and brick repair
Tony Devine, Renvers Restoration, Coach Lodge, Rathgar Avenue, Dublin 6, tel (01) 492 0292
Fleeton Watson Ltd, 63 Baldoyle Industrial Estate, Dublin 13, tel (01) 832 6994
Mowbray Ltd, 10 Drogheda Street, Balbriggan, Co. Dublin, tel (01) 841 1060
Seamus Wherity, Grougha, Balbriggan, Co. Dublin, tel (01) 841 3261
Wallpapers
Pat McBride, Studio 64, IDA Tower Pearse Street, Dublin 2, tel (01) 670 7984
David Skinner, The Mill, Celbridge, Co. Kildare, tel (01) 627 2913
Wood joiners and carvers
Acanthus Woodcarvers, Unit D, Aughrim Lane Ind. Est., Dublin 7, tel (01) 868 3035
Advance Joinery, 8a Henrietta Lane, Dublin 1, tel (01) 872 2066
Michael Behan, Painstown, Downdea, Co. Kildare, tel (045) 868 228
W. J. Bolger, (Ventrolla), 18 Ardee Street, Dublin 8, tel (01) 453 0377
Box Sash Window Co., Valerio, Mount Merrion Avenue, Blackrock, Co. Dublin, tel (01) 283 6943
Breffni Ltd, Main St, Ballinagh, Co. Cavan, tel (049) 37802
Charles Joinery, Main Street, Blessington, Co. Wicklow, tel (045) 865 149
Paul King, 142 Alpine Heights, Clondalkin, Dublin 22, tel (01) 457 0656
Paul Lawrence 50 North Great Georges Street, Dublin 1, tel 087 458203
Wlodak Szustkiewiz, The Mill, Celbridge, Co. Kildare, tel (01) 627 0548

Select Bibliography

Andrews, C. S. (Todd) *Dublin Made Me* Dublin, 1979

Barry, Michael *Restoring a Victorian House* Dublin, 1988

Burnett, John *A Local History of Housing 1815–1985* London, 1986

Bowen, Elizabeth *Seven Winters: Memories of a Dublin Childhood* London, 1942

Coolahan, John *Irish Education* Dublin, 1981

Costello, Peter *James Joyce: The Years of Growth 1882–1915* London, 1992

       with Tony Farmar *The Very Heart of the City* Dublin, 1982

       with John Wyse Jackson *John Stanislaus Joyce: The*
       Voluminous Life and Genius of James Joyce's Father London, 1997

Czira, Sydney *The Years Flew By: The Recollections of Madame Sydney Czira* Dublin

Daly, Mary E. *Dublin: the deposed capital, 1860–1914* Cork, 1984

Department of Environment, *Conservation Guidelines* Dublin, 1996

Dickinson, Page L. *The Dublin of Yesterday* London, 1926

Dillon, Eilis 'A Victorian Household' in Tom Kennedy (ed.) *Victorian Dublin* Dublin, 1980

Dublin Main Drainage Scheme Souvenir Handbook Dublin 1906

Dunlevy, Mairead *Dress in Ireland* London, 1989

Farmar, Tony *Ordinary Lives* Dublin, 1995

       Heitons—A Managed Transition Dublin, 1996

       Holles Street—the National Maternity Hospital 1894–1994 Dublin, 1994

Findlaters *Ladies Housekeeping Book* Dublin, 1896

Fox, R. M. *Louie Bennett* Dublin, 1957

Handyman, Christina *From Mangle to Microwave* Cambridge, 1990

Harrington, Kevin 'A Dublin Tragedy of 1861', in *Dublin Historical Record*, Vol. 35 pp 52–4

Hearn, Mona *Below Stairs* Dublin, 1993

Irish Georgian Society *The Conservation Directory.*

Johnston, Denis 'The Dublin Trams' in *Dublin Historical Record*, Vol. 12 pp 99–113

Joyce, James 'The Dead' *Dubliners* London, 1914

Kelly, Deirdre *Four Roads to Dublin: A History of Ranelagh, Rathmines and Leeson Street* Dublin, 1995

Little, F. J. 'A Glimpse at Victorian Dublin' in *Dublin Historical Record*, Vol. 6 pp 8–24

MacGiolla Phadraig, Brian 'Dublin One Hundred Years Ago' in *Dublin Historical Record* Vol. 23

McCarthy, Michael J. F. *Five Years in Ireland 1895–1900* London/Dublin, 1901

Nesbitt, Ronald A. *At Arnotts of Dublin* Dublin, 1993

O'Brien, Joseph V. *Dear Dirty Dublin* Berkeley/Los Angeles/London, 1982

O'Dwyer Frederick *The Architecture of Deane and Woodward*, 1998.

Pearson, Peter *Dun Laoghaire Kingstown* Dublin, 1981

Ross, John *Pilgrim Script* London, 1927

Smithson, Annie, M. P. *Myself and Others*, Dublin, 1944

       'Christmas in old Dublin' in *Dublin Historical Record*, Vol 6. pp 1–7

Tynan, Katherine *Twenty-Five Years* London, 1913

Williams, Jeremy *A Companion Guide to Victorian Architecture in Ireland 1837–1921* Dublin, 1994

Wilson, Laura *Daily Life in a Victorian House* London, 1993

Index